Rx for Learning Disability

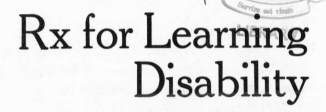

Rx for Learning Disability

Emmett Velten
Carlene T. Sampson

Nelson-Hall
Chicago

Illustrations: S/SGT. Stewart E. Ellison, U.S. Marine Corps

Library of Congress Cataloging in Publication Data

Velten, Emmett
    Rx for learning disability

        Bibliography: p. 155
        Includes index.
        1.   Learning disabilities.   I.   Sampson, Carlene T.,
    joint author.   II.   Title.
    LC4704.V44   371.9'14   77-8595
    ISBN 0-88229-330-3   (cloth)
    ISBN 0-88229-559-4   (paper)

Manufactured in the United States of America.

Contents

Preface

WE WISH THIS guide could become outdated soon, that the problem of educating the learning-disabled child could be resolved quickly and easily. That's not going to happen, but there are some favorable signs that help is on the way for the teacher. Workers in the field are developing educational programs based on careful analyses of learning tasks. Others are researching methods of finding out which children simply cannot be expected to profit from conventional group-instruction techniques. All this takes time, and meanwhile you have to use the best strategies you can for effective teaching. Here and there tools and techniques are available for the teacher who has a problem pupil and who needs to select an appropriate goal, break the learning task down into its steps, and make the individual modifications in teaching required to take the steps.

You won't find this guide a complete cookbook, though we do offer as many recipes as we can. Our main aim is to offer firm footing for that first step you may need to take toward your goal of providing some kind of help for the hard-to-teach child who is now sitting in your room discouraged, unhappy, and a burden on your conscience.

We address this book to teachers, but psychologists, read-

ing specialists, special educators, regular educators, adminis-
trators, curriculum specialists, principals, parents, and others
can use it just as well. All of us who encounter and help the
LD child are in the same boat, but the LD children aren't. We
will talk more about that later.

1. Our Approach

As TEACHERS OR other guiders of children you may have already read and heard plenty about a type of child who does not learn well with regular teaching methods. That is the child who is variously called "dyslexic," "perceptually handicapped," "minimally brain-damaged," "learning-disabled," and a mishmash of other terms all of which refer more or less to the same situation: namely, the child is not learning at his age or grade level, a failure that can't be blamed on mental retardation, underachievement, previous teachers, you, the parents, or primary emotional problems. The trouble may affect reading, writing, spelling, arithmetic, speech, listening, or more than one area. For our purposes, we will call such children learning-disabled, since this term refers most closely to the problem as you, the teachers, see it. Our bet is that these children will someday come to be called "teaching-disabled" or at least "learning/teaching-disabled" and we will have LTD-ers instead of LD-ers.

Already the term learning disability is falling into disrepute. Its popularity has led to its becoming a catchall, and worse, a cop-out for not teaching potentially teachable children. It is becoming the justification for building a bulky bureaucracy with expensive gadgetry from LD merchandisers. State legislatures and local school boards are getting on the bandwagon and steamrolling through special education programs for the learning-disabled. The frequency of descriptions of learning disability in popular publications such as *Better Homes and Gardens* (Knox, with Keisler, 1974) has been mounting of late, and the epidemic of LD-ism has spread faster than the Hong Kong flu ever did.

LD-ism is here and there being carried to the absurd, with some school systems applying the label to 100 percent of their pupils. Learning disability is being implicated by some in digestive problems, bed-wetting, long hair, hair-twiddling, murder, divorce, alcoholism, slums, living in sin, and the rise in violent crime, to name but some of its supposed results (see Divoky, 1974, by all means). Sterilization has even been suggested as a remedy for the evil of LD!

Sharp criticisms of these bizarre extremes of blame are in print now and promise to proliferate (Divoky, 1974). We endorse constructive and protective criticism of that sort, and we do the same here, but the fact remains that there are children who don't learn well by regular methods. We might as well call them learning-disabled if nothing else seems to apply.

By and large, learning disability is just a tarted-up term referring to a child's relative lack of learning from your standard procedures. Right away you can see that *you* are implicated in the child's having learning disability. It is not a disease, and it is not a medical term even when hidden behind aliases like "minimal brain damage" (a current favorite), or its less alarming version, "minimal brain dysfunction." Hardly ever can any damage be demonstrated, and in many of those instances where it can be, there is no disability in learning (Simensen and Sutherland, 1974). Damage *may* be there, or at least peculiar "wiring" of the brain, but for all intents and purposes, so what? Unless the damage is progressive, as in the case of a tumor, it is irreversible. Medication may help indirectly by making the child more attentive, and it is not to be despised, but it is not a panacea. "Smart pills" have yet to be invented, and medication does not cure even genuine brain damage, though it can prevent seizures and do a variety of other good things.

According to Bryant (1972), the percentage of school children who have this "LD" trouble is usually estimated to range from two or three to twenty-five. The estimated percentage depends on where the line is drawn between what is sufficient for passable classroom performance and what is not. In studies of this trouble, the most common percentage of children who are said to be learning-disabled is between seven and ten (Cruickshank, 1977).

Learning disability is often considered to be "inside" the child. In fact, there are reasons to believe it is partially, maybe even largely hereditary (Boder, 1971; Critchley, 1970). For one thing, it is consistently found that almost four times as many boys as girls have the trouble and it does seem to run in families. Be that as it may, something can still be done about it. Cause and treatment have no logical connection in learning disabilities and the treatment is "outside" the child. There is no way to sugar the pill: you, gentle reader, carry out the treatment.

In the past, you teachers have had several frustrations arising from your experiences with learning-disabled children. *First*, of course, is the frustration you feel as a professional since the pupil is not learning what you are teaching. *Second*, there is the frustration you feel as a person when the pupil and his parents have conferences with you, and as time passes and the pupil does not, you see them harden and begin to give up. The *third* frustration is fairly new and unexpected since it stems from the actual attempts to remedy the first and second frustrations and to help the afflicted pupils. It has to do with what happens in the school system when you refer your learning-disabled pupil for a psychological assessment. Typically you receive a report which does one of two things: (1) It may simply say the child is dyslexic (or whatever, including learning-disabled) and advise placement in a special class. If your system has a special class for such children, on the waiting list he goes and in your class he sits until an opening appears. This handles the problem in a certain type of way—for one child (who is probably still in your room). But what about your other two pupils who have the same type of trouble, but less so, or whose parents were leery of a psychological? (2) You receive a report which states that the child actually suffers from, say, poor auditory sequencing or poor figure-ground discrimination—which is something of a surprise to you since you thought he was a terrible speller and reversed letters—and proceeds to prescribe a series of strange exercises involving, for example, the pupil's learning to repeat progressively longer lists of digits and nonsense words or learning to trace pathways in mazes. The expectation is that the pupil's poor classroom performance on spelling and his reversals will change favorably after working with the "actual" (underlying) problems like auditory sequencing or figure-ground discrimination. Unhappily enough, it is beginning to look as if training in these supposed underlying processes does very little, sometimes nothing, to improve spelling and eliminate reversals, to continue our examples (Black, 1974; Cohen, 1969; Hammill, 1972; Johnson, 1974; Mann, 1970; Money, 1966). Besides that, the pupil is farther behind than ever in academics by the time he is proficient in repeating lists of nonsense words and tracing mazes, if in fact it has transpired that you or anyone else has had the time to spend teaching him these "skills." This can be quite frustrating and may not encourage you to refer any other pupils for psychologicals. It could be worse, however; some school systems do not even have anyone to whom to refer learning-disabled pupils.

ASSUMPTIONS

In this guide we take a different approach from that which has caused the third frustration above. Our initial and most important assumption is that *the theories about learning disabilities have become, for the most part, so much hoopla and we have gotten all the mileage out of them we are going to.* (For descriptions of the major theories, see McCarthy and McCarthy, 1969.) *The name of the game nowadays and in the foreseeable future is results.* If you read these theories closely you will notice that few of them have anything to do with whether particular remedial procedures work for any real-life problem (Cowgill, Friedland, & Shapiro, 1973). However useful learning-disability theories may have been for psychologists in the past, effective remediation has largely become a seat-of-the-pants operation, and will continue to be so, because it addresses everyday problems that demand solutions in fact, not in theory.

The abandonment of theory to see what really works is

good sense if not test-tube-pure science. Theory has worn it-self out in learning disabilities, and techniques of remediation must be the focus, perhaps even in the long run, for building a true scientific theory. The modern learning-disability specialist tries to figure out what will work and then, if he or she is theory minded, meditates on ways to explain it if it does. Theory will stem mainly from techniques and materials invented by close-to-the-situation observers such as you, the teachers, and by the badgered school psychologists who haven't been able to hide from you in the central office. Artists and electricians and mechanics and illustrators, among other "technologists," invent new equipment and materials, too. New materials create fresh opportunities for use and increase teachers' and psychologists' willingness to use them. The speed with which new materials get publicized causes progress in practice that theories cannot keep up with. This is just as well so long as the technologists keep their noses clean by promoting inventions that work, rather than hustling whatever it looks as if school systems and individual teachers and psychologists can be enticed into buying.

As learning disability becomes more the vogue in ed biz, let the buyer beware as he or she passes through the danger zone of materials catalogs. Trial and error is a reliable path to discovering what does work, but more than that is possible. When you read the brochure proclaiming the arrival of some new whiz-bang device, do not be overawed by pretty colors, high-octane terms, and trumpeted claims of virtue. If the ad lists a dozen school systems which have used Brand X, write them: Brand X may have failed miserably in them all or given such mixed results that investment of your money is unwise. Then again, you may receive vigorous positive testimonials. Above all, try to visualize your real-life learning-disabled pupils and their specific difficulties, and then consider closely whether it seems reasonable that the advertised device could or would help enough or at all.

Our second assumption, which follows from the first, is that *the learning-disabled pupil's problem is what you, the teachers, observe it to be.* If he can't spell, that is the problem, not, say, poor auditory-visual-motor association or something else you never heard of and would be of little use to you if you had. Learning disabilities itself is just a name for the problems you see with your eyes or hear with your ears in a pupil's academic performance. The name is shorthand for a whole lot of different things you see and hear and which would be too much trouble to list each time you want to refer to them. There is no generally accepted definition of the term (Wiederholt, 1974). The name only exists for convenience in communication, but we do need it. The name itself and other abstract terms are of minor help, however, when it gets down to doing something about the problems you see and hear. This is what we mean when we say that the learning-disabled child's problem is what you observe it to be and not something highfaluting from a theory, like auditory-vocal sequencing, which is just a high-level abstraction (Hoephner, Stern, & Nummedal, 1971) that has little or no connection with what goes on in your or anyone else's classroom.

Our third assumption is that *the report you, the teachers, receive should tell you specifically what to do for your learning-disabled pupil in terms of reasonably recognizable and commonsense procedures.* The report should not advise something esoteric like learning lists of nonsense words, tracing mazes, walking beams, or any rigamarole of the sort. The report and its follow-up should tell you what to do, what to do it with, and how to know whether you've done it correctly.

The psychologist's job is to translate his or her findings into terms you clearly understand and can do something with. If, after a careful reading, you do not know what to do with the report, then the psychologist, not you, has failed, and you should make this fact known in no uncertain terms. Your task is enough without having to learn a foreign tongue to boot.

Several things become clear given those three assumptions. In making your referral you need to *be as specific as possible in telling your school psychologist just how the learning-disabled pupil is having trouble*. The best way to do this is to provide samples of his work and have the school psychologist observe you and the pupil in action. This sharpens your own observations and you may find areas of strength in the pupil's work you had not previously noticed, or you may be able to put your finger on a very select area of trouble (such as, say, inability to distinguish short *a*, *e*, and *i*) which you had first seen as much more general (child can't learn phonics). You also should *give your psychologist a rough listing of the priorities* among a referred pupil's problems. In other words, in making the referral you need to let the school psychologist know just what the target is if he or she is to have a chance of hitting it and of being of use to you.

Another thing which begins to become clear, given the assumptions underlined above, is that frequently a great deal of the fancy material or placement in a special class is not what the learning-disabled pupil needs. Instead, *he needs you to teach him in a different way*. If the pupil has not been learning by regular methods, then he does need something different and individualized, not more of the same; this only stands to reason. And, let's face it, times being what they are, the only professional around who can absolutely be counted upon to be around is you, the regular classroom teacher. If the pupil doesn't get help from you, most likely he will not get it at all. We do have some ideas below, however, on resources you can use, and we most emphatically are in favor of special classes for the more severely learning-disabled.

Another implication of our assumptions underlined above is that *each child's problem is something different.* While general categories of disability exist, they are too general to be much use. A customized prescription for each learning-disabled pupil is needed. We give a great many suggestions below, but always there is something special to be added in individual cases. Most often you yourself will be adding this something special, so *you must maintain an experimental frame of mind.* Flexibility is the very heart of successful remediation.

2. Characteristics
of the
Learning-Disabled

WE PROVIDE THIS chapter to review some of the characteristics variously attributed to the learning-disabled. Some readers may not be too familiar with the LD area, so our grocery list may help them find out what to shop for. It is impossible to give such a list without its being shot through with the implication that kids with any or all of those characteristics have "got" something—something like a disease, a disease which leads to a label (diagnosis), a label which all too often leads to the kids' not being taught because it is erroneously proclaimed that they are practically unteachable except by the supertrained. That conclusion happens to be untrue, and that's why we've written this book. Here is a list of fifteen frequently mentioned characteristics of the hard-to-teach children called learning-disabled. The sixteenth characteristic is one which applies to certain sections of the nation more than others.

Specific Learning Disabilities

Learning-disabled children always have this characteristic; without it, they cannot be called learning-disabled. Some or all of the other characteristics enumerated below may be present, but most of them usually are not. This one, by definition, always is. Reading, writing, spelling, arithmetic, speaking, and listening may one or all show various deficits, gaps, or odd patterns. This is what is meant by specific learning disabilities. It is a detailed way of saying just how the pupil is hard to teach.

Reading and writing by the learning-disabled may show reversals, substitutions, omissions, or be agonizingly messed up, disordered, slow, mirrored, or almost absent despite apparent good sense on the pupil's part and definite effort on yours. Similar patterns of disability, gaps, or total incomprehension may be present in arithmetic. Speech may be halting or "funny" and listening a disaster area, with poor memory and apparent misperceptions. The child may have learned to talk late, at three or four, and may continue to mispronounce words. Usually, though, the child's learning disabilities lie in reading, writing, spelling—the three tend to hang together, particularly in the more severely disabled—or arithmetic.

The learning-disabled child may be poor in written work and may avoid reading like the plague, but he may participate with intelligent oral questions and answers; he may show unusual interest in drawing and mechanical things. Sometimes of course the clues to learning disability are more subtle, as when a child does normally well in writing phonetic words, even if fairly unfamiliar, but is at a loss on nonphonetics. Some LD children make astonishingly bizarre attempts at phonetic spelling on almost all words.

CONCEPTUAL AND PERCEPTUAL DEFICITS

The pupil may have difficulty in analyzing problems, in abstracting, generalizing, classifying, making educated guesses, and in evaluating results. If anything gives him more trouble than breaking the whole down into parts, it's putting it together again. Drawing, writing, and even copying may be poor. More likely, copying will be better than spontaneous writing. The child may have trouble staying on the line, between the lines, or anywhere in relation to the lines consistently. Figures may show numerous erasures, rotations, disorientations, disproportions, lack of closure, sketchiness, or otherwise be cockeyed. All of these "conceptual and perceptual deficits" are things you will observe for yourself, not from results of "perceptual" tests.

GENERAL COORDINATION DEFICITS

The LD child's overall bodily movement may look awkward, one-sided, jerky, or clumsy. Accident-prone, he may be the bull in the china shop of your crafts center, and at recess he may get hit a lot with the ball. Fine movements involved in writing, cutting, pasting, folding, hammering, stringing beads, working with puzzles, and so on, may look immature and clumsy. He seems to have poor ability to combine movement and vision.

VISUAL INEFFICIENCY

This characteristic is related to general coordination deficits. The LD child may show difficulty in focusing his eyes, in holding or finding his place on the page or chalkboard, and he may be a poor judge of distance. All this may be true even with 20/20 vision. A report that "his eyes are perfect" should be taken with a grain of salt if you notice any of the following signs:

    a) Head turning instead of eye movements
    b) Frequent loss of place on printed materials
    c) Frequent omissions of words and phrases
    d) Repetitive omissions of the small words
    e) Confusion of left and right
    f) Uphill or downhill writing (or both) even on lined paper
    g) Poor orientation of drawings on the page
    h) Stumbling or clumsiness in playground or classroom activity

HYPERACTIVITY

The LD child may be restless, overactive, readily bored, on the move. Some part or all of his body may be in constant motion. Such "driven" behavior may also be seen in excessive talk, unorganized thinking, inability to settle down to a task, even destructiveness. Not all hyperactives are learning-disabled and *vice versa,* but there is usually thought to be a significant overlap. Careful investigation recently, however, has suggested that LD-ers as a group are not any more hyperactive than "normals" (Bryan, 1974).

SHORT ATTENTION SPAN, DISTRACTIBILITY, POOR MEMORY

This characteristic is related to hyperactivity. The learning-disabled child may be unable to concentrate on one thing long enough to suit instructional purposes and is easily bored. He may be attracted to too many sights and sounds around him and be unable to adapt to them to screen out the irrelevant ones. Every movement, every color, every sound, every crosscurrent in the classroom may divert him from his work.

Poor Listening Ability

This characteristic is related to short attention span, distractibility, and poor memory. The learning-disabled child's memory for what he has heard may seem lacking and incorrect. He often cannot distinguish similar sounds one from the other, such as *b* and *t*, *v* and *th*, so of course he cannot attach correct pronunciations to their symbols and his spelling may be dreadful. Since much of what you and others say seems to him to be nonsense, his motivation to listen declines. At times you are bound to feel he is the one who hid behind the door when they were passing out brains because he thought they said trains.

Impulsivity and Poor Judgment

These characteristics are part of the hyperactivity, short attention span, distractibility, poor memory, poor listening ability package. The LD child may act without restraint, become overstimulated easily, hitting back and acting on immediate emotions, with little evidence of profiting from experience. He may not be able to keep from touching and handling objects, especially in novel situations, where he may really run wild. His speech may be brash and uncontrolled.

Excitability and Rage

This characteristic often goes with the general hyperactivity package. The learning-disabled child may have low frustration tolerance and may explode or become upset with minimal provocation. Though there will be good days, on the bad ones he may be irritable, touchy, aggressive. The child may not particularly remember his outbursts after they subside. In general, his behavior may be inconsistent, unpredictable, and pins and needles for you.

Laterality, Idea of Left and Right, Sense of Direction, Self as Reference Point

The learning-disabled child may have mixed laterality with, for example, dominant left eye, right hand, and left foot. Probably much more important a characteristic of the LD child is his inability or difficulty in remembering which is left and right. His sense of direction may be poor. He may have trouble with up and down, before and after, be a mess on maps and graphs, and hopelessly lost in the hallways of your larger schools. Idea of left and right and sense of direction both appear related to the child's ability to use himself as his reference point. If you face him and Simon Says, "Raise your right hand," he may raise his left, and when you gradually turn around with your back to him, he will be dumbfounded at seeing that you two are in fact holding up different hands.

ANXIETY AND POOR SELF-CONCEPT

Anxiety refers to nervousness rather than to hyperactivity and is usually a product of the failure the learning-disabled child experiences. Naturally there are many nervous ones who are not learning-disabled, and there is no connection between the two except when failure leads to nervousness. After enough time passed as a failure, the child thinks of himself in that dim light, and this is "poor self-concept." Once anxiety and poor self-concept get established, they act to impede further learning. The learning-disabled child, like everybody else, expects that what has been happening is what is likely to continue to happen, so his discouragement and frustration are understandable.

DAYDREAMING

In the learning-disabled, and of course they are only a minority of the daydreamers, daydreaming is a product of inability to follow what is going on in the classroom.

SPEECH

The learning-disabled child's speech may be halting, as a counterpart of his halting reading, or it may be nonstop as part of the hyperactivity package described above.

PERSEVERATION

This term means the child keeps on at a task or effort after the normal stopping point has been passed. You say, "Number to ten," and he keeps right on to the bottom of the page. He may repeat a letter, a portion of a drawing, a sound, or something else.

BILINGUALISM

From our personal experience here in the Southwest we have observed what we call "bilingual learning disability." We are not talking about children who simply do not know English well (or at all) because their early experience was with Spanish or an Indian language. We are talking about those who may have begun with a nonEnglish language or who were raised with two languages and who can speak English okay. *Some* of those latter youngsters appear to be messed up in some more enduring way in reading, spelling, and writing (but usually not in arithmetic), and we think this disability would apply to their work in Spanish or an Indian language as well as in English. Possibly this *results* from some type of conflict between the two languages which slows down the youngster's verbal responses. Then again, these may simply be children who have *regular* learning disability, but we see so many bilinguals that we erroneously conclude the disability stems from bilingualism. Whichever is the case, there are bilinguals with real learning disability and not just lack of knowledge of English. Distinguish between the two.

ATYPICAL PSYCHOLOGICAL TEST PERFORMANCE

As a characteristic of the learning-disabled, this is last and, for your purposes, least. Not because the learning-disabled aren't "picked up" on these tests, for they almost invariably are. This fact makes psychological test performance a close second to specific learning disabilities in identifying the learning-disabled. Psychological test performance is unimportant to you, however, because the results generally do not translate automatically into anything useful to you. So why should you have to pore over them like so many tea leaves? The school psychologist may choose to give certain tests to the child you refer. If he or she does so and has any consideration at all, the report spares you the jargon and moves swiftly from stating the name of the test to stating what it all means, instructionally speaking. Remember, the psychologist's job is to help you and your pupil, not to write high-sounding shoptalk, and if you let him or her do the latter, then you aren't doing your job either.

Being psychologists, we can say all this with impunity, but we do consider testing highly important and almost indispensable. Testing gives the psychologist clues as to which teaching tactics and materials are most likely to be profitable. It may also suggest the problem is not learning disability, but one of immaturity—where the child entered school too early —or limited intelligence or so-called cultural deprivation, each of which requires different sorts of remedies. What should be dispensed with is our tendency to write reports to ourselves rather than to you, the consumer.

One further word about testing. Do not be dismayed that tests come and go. Learning disabilities is a young field and much reworking of tests and jettisoning of certain others can be expected to take place. Most of you probably have heard, for instance, of the Marianne Frostig Developmental Test of Visual Perception (Frostig, Lefever, & Whittlesey, and Maslow 1966). Once an absolute must, for various technical reasons it is now used only with discretion. It does not measure what it purports to measure. Worse, the attendant remedial activities usually do not lead to improvement in the academic performance of children (Black, 1974; Mann, 1970). It may be a thing of the past someday, but no one years hence will ever question its value in having helped us get to some better place.

3. Remedies for Commonly Mentioned Tie-Ins with Learning Disability

In Chapter Two we discussed fourteen characteristics (excluding specific learning disabilities and atypical test performance) which the learning-disabled child might have but which he does not have by definition. He only has *specific learning disabilities* by definition. A question must be dealt with here: If the learning-disabled child has any of these nondefinitional characteristics, can specific remedies for them help remedy the learning disability itself? As we discuss these characteristics, you might glance back at each section in turn.

Conceptual and perceptual deficits are highly abstract names for some of the troubles you observe in the learning-disabled pupil's work. We do not believe these terms very useful in remediation because they are hopelessly far from classroom reality. They are mostly used in theories which advise maze-tracing, beam-walking, and similar noninstructional activities. If the child cannot keep his writing on the line, *that* is the problem and that is what the remedy should aim at, not "perception." This example illustrates that we always attempt to reach a specific instructional target. We discussed conceptual and perceptual deficits in Chapter Two since they are terms you will encounter in reading about learning disabilities. They do communicate a certain meaning, though not one we consider very important to remediation.

With general coordination deficits much the same holds true; the term is not too pertinent instructionally. Beam-walking and other training in gross and fine coordination certainly help the child become less clumsy, which is much to be desired. For that reason, if no other, it should sometimes be carried out. There is no evidence it automatically leads to, say, better spelling, however. Yet, if you work with the child on specific coordination deficits such as clumsy writing or cutting or pasting, you do help with specific instructionally relevant performances which, if improved, will help the child generally in the classroom.

With visual inefficiency the answer is that working on this can help remedy the learning disability itself. Remember, we are not talking about visual acuity here; obviously any child who cannot clearly see the chalkboard or page may profit from sharper vision provided by glasses. We are talking about types of vision problems which may exist with 20/20 acuity, such as difficulty in focusing or coordinating the eye movements. A vision specialist, an ophthalmologist or optometrist, is needed to make the appropriate examination. If you notice some of the visual inefficiency problems listed in Chapter Two, you might advise the child's parents to contact a vision specialist. Explain to them that it could be a problem not detected in routine vision examinations. In the classroom you can help the pupil in his efforts at effective use of his eyes by making his reading material vivid and rewarding. Straightedges under lines of print and window-slot cards (Chapters Ten and Eleven) also are helpful in this.

Hyperactivity, short attention span, distractibility, poor memory, impulsivity, poor judgment, excitability, and rage all tend to hang together and really amount to various degrees of the same thing looked at in different ways. We have divided them for convenience. Not every child with this hyperactivity package of troubles is learning-disabled and *vice versa* (Bryan, 1974), but any child who can be helped to have less of this hyperactivity package will probably show an increase in the amount of teaching he absorbs. He is not any smarter; he just pays attention better. Medication, usually stimulants such as Ritalin (among many others—we have heard good anecdotal reports on coffee!), is commonly used for reducing hyperactivity and increasing attentiveness. It can help the LD child if he also shows the hyperactivity package. The usefulness of these drugs tends to die out when the child reaches eleven or twelve, which, happily, is the time hyperactivity tends to diminish. If you are against such drugs, that is your business and has nothing to do with their effectiveness, which is unquestionable in a high percentage of cases (Conner, Eisenberg, & Barcai, 1967; Cutts and Jasper, 1949; Eysenck and Rachman, 1965; Lindsley and Henry, 1962; *Physician's Desk Reference,* 1973, 1972). Let the parents and the physician decide.

Quite likely, medication is coming to be too commonly used. The last thing a free society needs is to dope up everyone who makes a disturbance. There is a distinction between the climbing-the-walls types and those who, while too active for your complete comfort, don't need to be drugged. Make that distinction. Put your two cents in if you think you need to (see Schrag and Divoky, 1975).

Counseling the child patiently and repeatedly that he is just one of many and must think before acting may help somewhat to curb hyperactivity. The "stop, look, and listen" technique (Palkes, Stewart, & Kahana, 1968) in which children are taught to stop and listen, and to look and think before they answer seems promising. Quiet routines and unstimulating study carrels are helpful also in reducing excitability. Those pupils who almost go into rages under pressure can be supplied with a quiet place to which they may retire voluntarily when they feel a spell coming on and where they can remain until they cool down.

Poor listening ability often is part of the hyperactivity package. Then again, it may be poor hearing, and referral to an audiologist may be in order after the school nurse has done the preliminaries. It may also be—we hesitate to use psychological shoptalk—poor auditory discrimination. The child may have trouble distinguishing similar sounds even though his hearing acuity is perfectly all right. The remedy has to do with presenting pairs of words to the child containing the confused sounds, which in turn may be determined by a psychological test. It is difficult to make this particular remediation procedure relate directly to classroom material. We discuss it more fully later, but not that fully, because of the sheer cussedness of working with auditory discrimination and because it quite possibly is not as much related to reading ability as once thought. Recent research has found no relation between poor auditory perceptual skills (including auditory discrimination), as measured by tests, and reading ability (Hammill and Larsen, 1974).

The foursome of laterality, idea of left and right, sense

of direction, and self as reference point are generally lumped together under some such grand heading as body image. Three of these we like and the fourth, laterality, we lump. The more research done on laterality, the less important it gets to be in relation to learning disability. Children with mixed laterality, for example, appear to have no more reading problems than those whose laterality is unmixed (Fletcher, 1967).

The idea of left and right clearly is crucial in reading, writing, and arithmetic, and may often be taught in terms of specific instructional situations. Right is important since vertical addition, subtraction, and multiplication problems begin on the right. There are ways to teach the difference between left and right and we are more specific about this later, especially in references to color-cuing. If the child knows the concepts of left and right, you can speed remediation of reversals and other disabilities. You can say such things as, "Look at that. A *b*'s round part is on the *right*. You just made a *d*. The *d*'s round part is on the *left*." This does not mean the child instantly knows left and right, but at least he can reach the correct conclusion after thought.

If the child does not know left from right and is reversing letters, you can use crutches. For example, put a picture of a boy on the wall to the right of the pupil who can't reliably distinguish *b* and *d*. The child is told that the round part of the *b* points to the picture of the boy. Quite a to-do is then made over the fact that boy and *b* have the same initial sound. On his left is placed a picture of a dog and the same procedure is used. Eventually the child may learn to watch his *b*'s and *d*'s. With much repetition he may learn to associate right with boy and left with dog. The acid test will come when he scoots his desk around and the pictures are not moved. With right-handed children you can also emphasize, "Does it (holding a pencil, for instance) *feel* right? Then it *is* your right hand," (assuming, of course, that it is).

Since left and right are determined by the position of one's body, the child must have a clear idea that he himself is the reference point. Reams of excellent material have been written on this (see, for example, Kost, 1972), and we will go into little detail here. Simple Simon games stressing left and right, labeling the parts of the body using a drawing of the front and a drawing of the back, and tying a ribbon on the wrist of the dominant hand are all helpful in establishing oneself as a reference point, in improving the ease with which the idea of left and right comes to mind, and in improving sense of direction.

Anxiety and poor self-concept may be products of learning disability, or rather the failure produced by learning disability. Helping the child with the specifics of learning disability may lessen his anxiety and improve his self-concept as he comes to experience success. Anxiety is decreased by having steady routines established for the pupil, too. High anxiety and pronouncedly poor self-concept may need to be dealt with by counseling or some other psychological treatment since they impede learning as well as feel bad in their own right.

Daydreaming, where it is a product of learning disability, will decrease when the child is able to participate more successfully in class because of your different teaching tactics. He will be able to participate more fully when you teach him in simple, short, appealing steps.

Halting or stumbling speech may become more fluent as the child learns to read with more ease, just as stuttering sometimes is reduced when the child's anxiety diminishes. Then again, halting speech may need to be dealt with by a speech therapist. Use your discretion here. The degree of the speech problem is the primary consideration, of course. If your school system has a speech therapist, he or she may also be able to give you tips on teaching things like vowel sounds. Brash speech or uncontrolled speech is part of the hyperactivity package.

If a child perseverates a lot, there are general tactics to help him learn not to. Usually it can be dealt with in the specific situation in which it occurs, such as numbering down the page. The best remedial procedure is simply blocking off the pupil's tablet after, say, ten lines and telling him that is where to stop. Similar mechanical devices to force a stop to the perseveration can be used in any other situations in which it occurs. Often you can teach the pupil to count how many of something he needs to write and to recheck to prevent himself from going too far. Perseveration is not a very important problem in most cases; mainly it serves as a clue that learning disability in general exists, so that you may look for more important specifics if you haven't noticed them before. We will say no more about it.

In bilinguals who have trouble learning, you want to make sure first it's not a matter of just not knowing English well enough. If a child does not know English at all or knows hardly any, we advocate that he be taught academic basics *in his native tongue*. Once the basics are firm in, say, Spanish, the child will be able to translate them into English as he begins to learn English. If he has to learn basic academic concepts and English at the same time, you're asking for trouble.

Many Southwestern school systems have ESL (English as a Second Language) programs, and these establish the academic basics in the child's native language. If your school system has no such thing, try to work with the child's parents through a translator so that the basics can be taught in the native language while you work on teaching English.

If the child is truly learning-disabled, that is, he has a bilingual history but knows English fairly well and is showing specific learning disabilities, then he needs plain old LD remedies just as do your pupils who were raised speaking English only. The tools and techniques in this guide apply to bilingual LD-ers too.

4. The Weak Links

IN THE PAST, what to do was the chief weakness in the diagnosis-treatment-improvement chain for helping learning-disabled children. This was partly because the diagnostic and prescriptive material which you, the teachers, received in your reports was incomprehensible. Often, too, the treatment procedures suggested were not specific enough and didn't really work if applied. We have discussed these frustrations above and suggested some remedies for them. We have suggested that you must observe carefully, be specific in describing the learning disability targets, give priorities, teach differently, and be experimentally minded. In his or her turn the psychologist must tell you almost exactly how to apply remedies and how to know whether you have done it. If he or she fails to do this, your further duty is a request for better help. We also pointed out that in most cases it is you, the regular classroom teacher, who is going to be doing the doing, since there are few special classes and often nobody much to be counted upon.

Other points are pertinent to the weak link problem. Sometimes it was not the psychologist's psychologese or the school system's lack of special classes. Sometimes it was you, gentle reader. Too often the teacher has felt his or her duty was over once a referral was made, particularly in those cases where the child has been such a trial that you are only too glad to wash your hands of him or have the illusion of so doing by making the referral. True handwashing cannot take place since the school psychologist only diagnoses and prescribes, while you carry out the treatment. Unless there is a special class, and usually there isn't, the child stays right there in your very own classroom. Unless you begin to teach him in a different and individualized way (maybe suggested in the report), he will sit there just as before the psychological assessment only rather farther behind academically than he was some weeks earlier when the referral process first cranked up. True, it would be nice, it would be desirable, it would be neat if someone else took over the learning-disabled child, but again and again the fact must be faced that, by and large, you're it. You owe it to the child, who is innocent as a babe, at least in not having elected to be learning-disabled (or to go to school, for that matter). Once you begin to cope with the learning-disabled, whatever else you may say, you will not say that your day is boring routine.

Furthermore, the old excuse about "I'd like to but I can't with thirty others" no longer cuts ice. Time and again, day in and day out, you already are teaching individual children. Whenever your pupils have individual assignments, whenever they are divided into tracks and levels and circles, whenever some are doing math and some reading and some working in

crafts and some running errands and some at your desk, whenever you answer one child's question or help another at his
seat or write an individualized comment on a homework sheet
like "Much better, but watch your signs!" whenever you do
any of this, which is every day, you are doing what is required
with the learning-disabled child, though with him it is done
in a more concentrated form. Fifteen or twenty minutes a day
of individual instruction can be easily managed if you are organized and know your goals, and it can make an enormous
difference for the child. The rest of his day can be spent in
preplanned seatwork which you check on from time to time.
All this is far easier if you have an aide or volunteer resource
person (see Chapter Fifteen), but you can do it yourself. You
can make other allowances too. If the child can't write yet, tell
him you know he can't, that he will someday, but till then you
will test him orally, so he should listen carefully.

Besides all that, helping the learning-disabled is not the
deep and tangled mystery old-time psychological reports and
most books on the subject lead you to believe. It is using crafty
teaching tactics designed always, one way or the other and bit
by bit, to overcome a difficulty that not only may frustrate
you for eight or nine months, but may cause heartache and
permanent defeat in a child and his parents. Don't be irritated
with the learning-disabled pupils, for they force you to do
your best teaching. They will teach you more than your regular pupils, not just in terms of techniques, but in patience and
persistence too.

You may be saying (we hope you are) that all this sounds
good—modestly so, at least—but tell us more. Already we
have anticipated ourselves and must go back to the point at
which you have first judged that a pupil is in fact learning-
disabled or very much seems so, and move forward again till
we reach the time when you are applying remedies in class.

5. What Do You Do First After You've Identified the Learning-Disabled Child?

THE ANSWER TO the question of the title is to make a referral or at least think about making one. A referral may be defined as preparing for and taking organizational action on the pupil's behalf, his parents', and yours against the problem as you have observed it. If yours is a school system or town where there is no one to whom to refer, do not despair by any means. True enough, it is a lonely feeling when you not only end up with the ball (as will be true even with most of the teachers who have referral resources galore), but have to carry it most of the game since there is no one else on the team but the parents. Still, with your wits about you, you can do a lot all by yourself if you are willing to experiment. Especially after you get the knack of it, a full-fledged referral may not always be necessary even where there is someone to whom to refer. We imply as much in the first sentence of this paragraph when we say ". . .

or at least think about making one." Careful observations of the sort preparatory to making a referral may suggest theretofore untried remedies to you. It may clarify the problem in such a way that you try one more tactic, and that one may work. We hope the various techniques, tricks, crutches, and so forth we trot out later in this guide will give you clues and inspiration to invent just what you need for your own situation. And indeed, the remedy generally will be individualized, so even if your school has a whole fleet of specialists, you yourself will be making the precise fit of their recommendations to your special situation.

But let us assume you do have a referral resource and follow that route. One of your pupils in particular is clearly not learning or producing in some important way. His work is not just dull or slow, but is peculiar. Looking back at Chapter Two of this guide, you feel quite sure his work shows specific learning disabilities, and his work or behavior may show other of the possible vexing characteristics as well. He seems smart enough—he knows everything about ants and there was that time he got the audiovisual equipment to work for you— so it's not that. He does try at least as hard at times as other kids who seem similar but who do much better work. Certainly his tortured efforts at spelling give every evidence of motivation. While he often does not look so happy in class, he isn't particularly shy and in the cafeteria he has enormous fun (perhaps more than is strictly desirable, in fact). So you tend to rule out emotional problems as causing the learning difficulty. You definitely recollect on Parents' Night his parents did not attend, and that makes you wonder.

You consult two sources at this stage. One is the cumulative record, which may bear out what you already know: the pupil's achievement is low and it didn't start just with you.

Has he repeated a grade? Also you may notice an IQ score that looks respectable. You note the parents' address and telephone number and divine what you can about the family. What do they do, where are they from, and are there cross references to testing files in the central office on other children in the family? Your other consultation at this stage is with last year's teacher, if available (unless you're the first one). Possibly you've already heard the full story in the teachers' lounge, but if not, informally tell last year's teacher about your situation with the pupil. Most of the time you will learn that it was just the same last year, only maybe not quite as bad because the material was easier. You might get valuable tips on what works too, but let's assume that last year's teacher was up the same tree you are. You feel confirmed in your view that action must be taken. The problem is bone deep and requires more than a Band-Aid.

It is time to talk with your principal. Tell him or her what your observations of the pupil are, what you have tried and with what result, and what promises to happen at promotion time if something beneficial doesn't intervene. Display some of the child's work. The principal most likely will be able to add to the picture with grapevine information and perhaps background material of this sort or that. Ask about making a referral to the school psychologist. If the go-ahead is given, gather the forms which need to be filled out. The larger your school system, the lengthier the forms are likely to be, but also the more likely will be the existence of resources to help you and the pupil. So, persist.

Then comes the decision about the parent conference. The principal and you may want to see the parents together, or it may be you alone. If you have not had several years of teaching experience, if you are at all unsure of your footing, if you have the slightest suspicion that ill feelings may emerge at the conference, have your principal with you. After all, he or she is in charge of curriculum, too, not just discipline and administration.

Whether it is you alone or you and the principal, your part of the conference and its lead-in will be much the same. We will only cover this territory once, though some of it may be more relevant to the telephone part and some to the in-person part. For starters, the best bet is a personal telephone call to the pupil's home in the evening, since there is more chance both parents will be home then. If there is no telephone, note-sending will have to be your method, which is really a bother since any teacher can testify to the tendency for notes to get lost. A home visit may be needed, or a telephone call to the parents' place of work.

But let us assume for now that there is a home telephone. Ask to speak to Mr. or Mrs., and whichever one you get, try to speak to the other one too. Introduce yourself and give every evidence of pleasantness and interest in the child. If you already know them this part will be easy, especially if you haven't let the situation go on so long that you view Johnny as a definite irritation and the parents then say, "Why didn't you tell us this sooner?" If that question does arise, a suitable reply will refer to your having needed time to make sure that you yourself were unable to fulfill your job of teaching their child adequately without additional help from a specialist, and that is what you are calling about.

Actually the parents probably know about their child's academic problem already if he has been in school before. Their worry and lack of satisfaction from some previous teacher may help explain their absence on Parents' Night. If you hear the didn't-give-us-satisfaction story about another teacher, listen, then switch back to the present. *Never* talk about another school or another teacher negatively. It will undermine the parents' confidence in you and your school. Rest assured that every word you say will find its way to the ears you would least desire to hear it. The chickens will come home to roost, like birds of doom, right over your head. This could be most unpleasant, especially if it occurs in that haven from care, your very own teachers' lounge.

At any event, and again this applies to telephone or in-person conversations, after your introduction and pleasantries with Johnny's parents, move right into the fact that they will have noticed that Johnny's grades, the papers he's taken home, and the various notes you may have written indicate a real problem with such and such. Assure them that his intelligence seems fine and that he tries, but somewhere there is a hang-up in the learning process, and you would like testing to show how he can get more out of his schooling. If you get this far without incident, and most likely you will, tell the parents what must be done to arrange the testing. Tell them who will do it and what it will cost (if anything). Emphasize that the results are confidential but will be discussed with them in full. In Arizona, school records are open to parents. Check the law in your locality. The parents will have to sign a release-permission form. If you have done all this by telephone, it is best for one or both parents to come in to school to sign the form. If they do, you can show them more of Johnny's work, they can see you and your classroom, and they can have a more personal conference with you and perhaps the principal. If the conference is held in your classroom, it is better, during the sitting part, for all of you to sit democratically and uncomfortably in tiny little chairs rather than for you to loom up and over the parents behind your desk. Establish a pattern for future contacts with the parents. They will be valuable allies. If the parents absolutely cannot come to the school, mail the relevant forms to them with a stamped, addressed, return envelope.

If the parents have no telephone and you send a note home by the child asking them to contact you or meet you at school, some will not respond. Follow the note with a letter, and keep a carbon. If you get no response then, confer with your principal about a home visit. You, the principal, the school social worker, the nurse, or the attendance officer may make the visit. If the visit is by someone other than you, prepare that person fully with information and forms. If the parents are not home, call again. You might leave a note telling them who you are, why you came, and when you will call again. We know of cases where parents hid and refused to answer the door, fearing who knows what?

Where the child needs special services and the parents will not or cannot cooperate, confer with your principal again. If you get his or her backing, confer with your local child neglect and abuse agency. A full-fledged complaint may not be merited or needed, but confer and find out. If a complaint is merited and needed, you, or more likely your principal, must do it. The child should not suffer because the parents don't care or because they are so problem-ridden or deprived that they cannot respond to the educational needs of their child. You will not meet that kind of bad situation often, but bad situations are dealt with best by knowing how to face them and then by doing so.

6. The Psychological Assessment and Follow-Up

WHEN ALL THE school forms and parent signatures have been secured, send them to your school psychologist and call him or her too if you can. Even though you will be seeing each other soon to examine the pupil's work together and have your first conference, early personal contact often speeds the process. You may get to know each other well before the year is out. You will get more work out of the psychologist if he or she feels you have a personal interest in helping facilitate the job. Also, the squeaking wheel gets the grease.

Each school psychologist will have a different way of working, but it is certain that he or she will need to see some of the referred pupil's work and probably keep some of it. It is nearly certain that the psychologist will want to observe in the classroom. Classroom observations are not disruptive if they are matter of fact. All you need to do, if that much (it depends on the frequency of observers in your class-room), is tell the children there will be a visitor, and by way of normal teaching routine put the referred pupil through his paces for the observer's edification. Of course give no indication that the observer is observing anyone or anything in particular. With conduct problem children whom you refer, there is a maddening tendency for them to be model pupils the one day the observer is present. There is little chance of this with the learning-disabled since self control hardly figures in that problem.

If the school psychologist decides on testing, and typically he or she will, it will be set up with your schedule and the school's in mind. With grammar-school children, testing is done mostly in the morning. If the pupil is absent on the scheduled day, let the psychologist know promptly if you can catch him or her before departure from the central office. Only the greener psychologists will fail to call ahead anyhow, but courtesy is always appreciated. For your part, try to think ahead regarding assembly programs, field trips, and the like, so that you will not be making a last-minute rescheduling call, or, alternatively, the pupil will not be missing something he has looked forward to with pleasant anticipation if you decide to go ahead with the testing regardless. Then again, there are many learning-disabled children who will walk over burning coals to get to the testing session if they see it as offering hope for eventual freedom from their burdens. Use your judgment; you can always ask the child.

Prepare the child for the testing session by telling him something like this, suitably modified as needed: "You know how different cars need different kinds of gas to run well?" (If he didn't, he does now!) "For some reason people are the same way. Some children, like you, don't learn their school work well with the teacher's regular teaching, so the teacher has to find a different way to teach them, and that's what I'm going to be doing with you. It doesn't mean you're not smart, because you are smart. You just don't learn well in the regular way. Anyhow, someone is going to come out to school before long to give you some interesting tests and stuff to find out what new way I may need to teach you. After that, it won't be long before I start to teach you in a different way so you can learn better and faster. How does that sound?" Answer his questions and he will be ready for the testing session when it rolls around.

The psychologist should tell you approximately when the testing and the subsequent report can be expected; this total time span should not exceed two weeks. Shortly after you have received a report, the psychologist should arrange a conference with you. In it the recommendations are discussed and ideas developed on how to implement them. If the report comes and you do not hear from the psychologist within the week, make a telephone call yourself to set up the conference. The old approach too often was for the psychologist to send the report and forget about you, but this is no longer acceptable. On the contrary, not just one conference, but a continuing follow-up must be conducted. Recommendations often fail to work or are inapplicable for reasons neither you nor the psychologist foresaw in your first post-test conference. Revisions may be called for. This is only to be expected and is nothing to worry about. You and the psychologist may have to experiment for a long time in tough cases before positive results begin to flow. Before it is discarded, you must give any particular recommendation a decent trial; otherwise you don't know what works or what doesn't.

The school psychologist will have to present the test results and general recommendations to the child's parents too. Often the psychologist will be able to help the parents understand the problem and give them concrete ideas on how to help their child, so that they no longer feel like helpless bystanders at the scene of an accident. Finally, the psychologist will have to present test results to the pupil. You share in this and in fact may lead the way and do most of it. Generally the approach is a repetition of the car-gas story. Soup it up a little if you can, and then move right into as accurate a description of your new teaching methods and materials as you can give. Emphasize that he must try his very best; give encouragement and assurances about his intelligence. The psychologist will already have planted motivational seeds during the test session itself. Any child knows an adult does not come out to the school and get him out of class to play games, so the test session is hardly ever described as games nowadays. The tests may be fun but their purpose is serious, and the child is told the purpose is to try to find out how to help him do better in school. Explained that way, the younger learning-disabled children typically are more than eager to cooperate both in testing and in remediation. With the older ones, say ten to twelve, a certain bit of sullenness begins to creep in, even as it would with you or anyone else subjected to four or five years of frustration and failure. At that age more attention will need to be devoted to developing and maintaining the child's motivation.

By junior or even senior high—and some of them get that far—dislike for school may be so deep and hope for academic success so lacking in him that the learning-disabled youngster might be lost to the academic educational world even if you had sure-fire instructional remedies. He may merely be existing, grimly waiting for the ticking clock to signal drop-out time. Such a youngster is no different from a learning-disabled second grader in his potential for profiting from individualized remediation, and in fact he may have more potential. His attitude, a product of his bad school experiences, is the stumbling block with the time server. A great deal of counseling may be necessary, and special vocationally-oriented courses of study may have to be arranged for the youngster to modify such attitudes. Surprisingly, there are some such older youngsters who are remarkably placid and gratefully accept remedial help. Try it and see (Goodman, 1973).

Let us return to the young learning-disabled child where there is every hope and where you can make a literal lifetime of difference for another human being through your efforts. Let us say you have identified the child, made the referral, recommendations have been produced, and you and the school psychologist are following through. What is needed now is diligent, individualized teaching. As we said above, you already are giving plenty of individualized instruction. Far from being the last straw, a little more such individualized teaching will benefit you enormously if set about correctly. It will remove boredom with its challenge. It will produce immense satisfaction in you and rejoicing in the child and his parents when success begins to show. Since you will be frankly committed to providing the best education for the disabled child, your commitment will grow to providing it for each child. Since there is such a range of children, your classroom organizational and management skills will increase. In short, instructing learning-disabled children can provide a real boost to your teaching. Study the material below, and you will see that instruction of the learning-disabled, at its core, is little more than particularly skillful and concentrated regular instruction applied to especially resistant problems. This is not to imply that it is cinchy and that all the answers are clear. Far from it, or we would not have labored over this guide and you would not be doing so either.

We will now turn to descriptions of the specifics for successful remediation of learning disabilities. We have set forth a good deal of material above for you to plow through, and we trust the point has been made that specifics rarely can be made specific enough in books since real-life situations so often differ from those in textbooks. That is why you need the experimental frame of mind and continuing use of your school psychologist in the follow-through.

We have tried to group our suggestions sensibly, but overlap is unavoidable. We begin with the conditions of the remediation process and then discuss the supremely important matters of motivation and discipline, two applied areas of behavior modification. We move on to the conditions of success, with sections on the characteristics of classroom organization, of instructions, and of materials. All of that deals with the arrangement of the learning environment and could be lumped into one giant chapter. We have divided it into three parts to make it easier to follow.

Reversals cut across so many areas and are so often cited as a learning disability that we assign it a whole section. We then get down to the brass tacks of crutches and cues, tactics and tricks, applied to particular academic areas. We provide some material for a few wall or desk charts of use to all your children, but more so to the learning-disabled. Then we give review lists of dos and don'ts useful to you in teaching and in conferences with parents of your pupils. Some of these dos and don'ts apply to behavior management and to homework and how parents can help with it more effectively. We make suggestions on resource people. Read all this material and decide what you can use as it is and what you can modify to suit your purposes.

7. Conditions of the Remediation Process

WE WILL NOW present three conditions for successful remediation which absolutely must be put into effect if you are to get positive results with your learning-disabled pupils. These conditions sometimes repeat or extend the key assumptions and their implications discussed in the material above. We present them in a different way here as we begin to get closer to particulars. But as we get closer, we still tend to fall short of being precisely what the doctor ordered for specific troubles. This is because there are at least as many remedies as there are cases of learning disability, since each case is to some degree different from others and thus calls for individualized recommendations and a tailored fit. We will try to help as much as we can, but remember, no book could ever tell you just what to do correctly and in every detail, in each case. This chapter, however, is one place where you will be told precisely what you must always do. When you meet with trouble in the remediation process, ask yourself whether you have precisely stated your goal. Ask yourself whether you divided the gap between pupil as-is and the goal into manageable steps. Ask yourself whether you know exactly how you plan to take the steps. Once you reanswer those questions, most likely the trouble can then be surmounted.

State the Goal

This is the first of the three conditions you must arrange after identifying the difficulty and enlisting the service of your school psychologist. The goal is to improve the final product, the pupil's demonstrated learning. *To reach any goal you must specify the goal precisely.* If you ask children to clean their desks and you find that little Suzie simply put her rubbish inside her desk out of sight, do not be too quick to rebuke. You would have done better to have spelled out exactly what you meant by a clean desk. That way profitless bickering of the but-you-didn't-say-to sort cannot occur.

In your personal affairs time and again you will find yourself thinking you must do better without any clear agreement with yourself of what better means objectively. How are you to know whether you have done that much better or not? What's to prevent you from remaining discouraged, even though you did show some slight improvement, because you really never thought to define "better" precisely enough so that you could be gratified when you got there? If you wish to lose weight, how much? How fast? By what kind of diet? What are your meals to be day by day? Realistically, how much chance are you going to have of sticking to your diet without a plan?

It is the same with learning disabilities. You do not just form the goal that your pupil spell better, but you decide just what you mean by better, as in "Know how to spell the first twenty-five words of the Dolch Basic Word List." That is the first condition necessary at this stage of the remediation process, stating the goal. It is no different from identifying the area of weakness, except a matter of degree. If a child is three years low in spelling, a realistic goal may not be three years of progress in one year, but perhaps a year and a half of progress. More realistic still is setting a goal for a particular week or even day. Stating the goal precisely means you can know whether you have reached it or not.

Divide the Gap Between Pupil As-is and the Goal into a Series of Small Steps

This is the second condition necessary for successful remediation. You must plan the parts of each remedial session, plan each day's learning tasks, and have weekly lesson plans as part of your overall program for the pupil. Often the steps need to be made smaller than first thought, so this stage requires flexibility in revamping your plan after you check your results. The fact of the matter is that with the more severely disabled pupils the steps may be minute, and you will call any progress at all a step forward. The goal sometimes moves back a bit toward pupil as-is too, but this is just part of the experimental frame of mind you need in such teaching. Programmed instructional materials incorporate these ideas of small, secure steps and knowing just how the learner rates at each step of the learning process. Make the steps in the remedial material for the learning-disabled pupil as much like programmed instruction as you can.

Decide How You Are to Take the Steps to Reach the Goal

Arranging this third condition is where the psychologist can be particularly helpful. In fact this should be the main thrust of his or her report. There used to be two main schools of thought on this matter. One, you identified weaknesses (here we mean the old-fashioned weakness terms such as poor auditory sequencing) and gave the pupil exercises to build up his weakness in that area so that advances in learning could flow. We hope we have already torpedoed this kind of theory. Progress, when based on the more esoteric remedial procedures, has typically been unforthcoming to any significant degree, as Mann (1970) and others have demonstrated. The second school of thought was to teach to strengths. This is much more sensible—you would not teach a homing pigeon to walk his message to its destination—but here too the strengths were too often glowingly extolled in directives like: "Utilize the kinesthetic modality," whatever that means.

Ultimately, both approaches were routinely recommended. You were advised to teach to strengths while eliminating weaknesses, which came to include everything but the kitchen sink. This had the singularly self-defeating result of doubling the length of reports to teachers. Only those with true bulldog tenacity could even wade through such cheerless long reports, much less do more than throw in the towel after having done so. We ourselves have written long reports in our day, more recently than we would care to admit, and felt mildly indignant that most of the recommendations were not followed, give or take a dozen. If the recommendations had been followed, the learning-disabled pupil might at least have shown some signs of blossoming, but only if the recommendations were carried out by the psychologist who wrote the report, for only he or she would know what the report was talking about. That the recommendations typically were not followed is what led us, to coin a phrase, to use psychology. We thus arrived at our three main assumptions (see Chapter One) whose purpose is to make reports understandable and aimed at precise targets, and, accompanied by personal follow-up, likely to produce desired results. Long, jargon-filled reports have become more and more streamlined, toned down, and tailored to teacher language and needs. This process necessarily led to acceptance of the position that the learning-disabled pupil's difficulty is what it is observed to be, that remedies must be sharpshooting applications of commonsense instructional procedures, and that experimentation is necessary. This new position is the practical school of learning-disabilities remediation.

In arranging the third condition for learning-disabilities remediation—deciding how to reach the goal—experimental teaching comes in. Essentially you, along with your school psychologist, try to think of ways by which the pupil can learn what he previously has not. The psychologist's test results, in all their psychologese glory, help a lot here. He or she in fact may discover that it *is,* judging from the tests, a problem of poor auditory discrimination, deficient visual memory, lack of kinesthetic associations to visual perceptions, or something of the sort, which will mean little to you but should help him or her cook up recommendations that will address the specific problem. These recognizable recommendations are duly made and team teaching by you and your school psychologist commences.

To take the steps to the goal and to do this teaching, you need to have at hand the tablets, colored pencils, graph paper, flash cards, straightedges, abacus, phonics kit, Cuisenaire rods, and any other necessary material. Know how to use these and have definite ideas of what to do when you meet obstacles. Have incentives which you can use to maintain the pupil's interest and effort. Now that you're ready to go, how can you get the pupil moving?

8. Motivation and Discipline

MOTIVATION SPRINGS FROM SUCCESS; lack of motivation results from failure. The learning-disabled child will have been failing, relatively speaking and perhaps absolutely, so his motivation may leave much to be desired, though sporadically he may try hard. Building up the child's motivation when he lacks the ability to express it in performance may frustrate him terribly. This is where your different teaching tactics must enter the scene, so that motivation can take the child along a different pathway around the disabling roadblock previously impervious to regular teaching.

Where do you start? First you determine the pupil's achievement level, which really amounts to specifying the difficulty, which you did early in the referral process. If he reads at the first-grade level, there is no use promising candy and privileges if he reads his third-grade book. Begin on the ground floor. Go back far enough to permit the child to succeed at every step. Make the steps small enough that success is unavoidable. If the child does not succeed, make the steps still smaller. Once a few steps and then some more are taken successfully, motivation begins to grow. Eventually a feeling of confidence may appear.

If the child will not take the first step, and many of the thoroughly defeated ones will not, use "artificial" rewards. There is no shame in this. We adults do not work exclusively for the joy of it. It is unrealistic to expect children to do so either, learning-disabled or not. We are talking about behavior modification techniques, and you can and should use these techniques all through the remediation process and with your entire class if you wish (Buckley and Walker, 1970; Ferinden, 1970; Hunter, 1967; Zifferblatt, 1970).

Little children may work for gold stars, smile faces, or (if you are not among the dentally devout) M & M's. All kinds of tiny trinkets, prizes, privileges, and praise may be effective rewards. Activity rewards may be determined by observing what the child likes to do in his free time. The exact type of reward can be worked out with your school psychologist and we cannot present a behavior modification manual here. We will say flatly that it always works; it is a matter of experimenting to find the effective technique. Reward each success in some manner. Make the child very conscious of success and progress. Graphs which show progress are very helpful, and the child may learn how to make the daily entries himself. Counsel with him about his progress, then mention areas where improvement is needed. Discuss your plan for helping him progress further.

Don't hitch your wagon to a gold star unless you have to, however (Greene and Lepper, 1974). If the kid gets a kick out of the work itself, don't distract him with gold stars, fatten him with M & M's, or glut his mind with graphs of his progress. Judge what you need to use by looking at his behavior. If he just sits there with your new work, specially tailored for him, you'd best unpack your behavior modification kit. If he's off and running with motivation from the learning tasks themselves, plus your encouragement, keep the kit in reserve. You may need it eventually, and with most LD-ers, you'll need it a lot and probably from the start. After years of failure at academics (and when you're seven or eight, one year is a lot), it'll take plenty of extrinsic motivators to get him going again. Use your discretion. Don't get a full-tilt behavior modification program underway unless it's required.

If a child fails something, let him try another activity. Make no comment regarding the failure unless he does. Simply tell him you will replan it so he can learn it, and then do so and return to it later. He has had enough frustration without adding to it the fear that he is failing on his very last chance. Approach the whole matter scientifically. If an automobile does not run after the mechanic's efforts at repair, whose responsibility is it to try again in a different way? The car's or the mechanic's?

Learning-disabled children need the three Fs of firmness, friendliness, and fairness on your part even more than the rest of the children do. Consistency will give the learning-disabled pupil a feeling of security and of belonging, so provide it. *Explicitly state your expectations for his behavior and for his completion of remedial work*. Tell him what will happen after he has finished, such as a reward, a change of pace, or what-have-you. Since he often is hyperactive or defeated or good at evading the work he failed in the past, the learning-disabled pupil needs firm authoritative guidance and discipline. Discipline does not mean punishment; rather, it means structure and timed rewards and other alternatives to traditional punishment, such as time-out (Gnagey, 1967; Madsen and Madsen, 1970).

We will describe one possible alternative to punishment, often called overcorrection or restitution, which we call "positive practice" (see Hill, 1963, for details of Guthrie's theory of learning). Positive practice cuts off the undesirable behavior, teaches the child the correct actions, and rewards him for taking them. Here is how to do it. Little Johnny paper-airplanes the pitifully meager completed portion of his assignment up onto your desk, possibly from quite a distance. If he ever gets that far, he may be a hotshot someday in junior high basketball, but you must deal with The Situation now, especially as other children either are giggling or have gone dead silent to watch your response. You stare icily at Johnny and with extreme firmness say, "Come get your paper. Take it back to your desk. Sit down." Naturally, you will be pausing as each of these steps is executed. "Now unfold your paper and fold it the correct way. Now get up and walk to my desk quietly. Put your paper on the pile neatly with the others. Go back to your desk and sit down. Thank you. You did all that very well." Permit the flicker of a smile to show, then switch it off for an especially firm, "Don't *ever* throw anything in this classroom again."

This procedure sets firm rules and gives the pupil practice in correct behavior and praise for it. The other children will be watching all this, mostly thunderstruck, but should one snicker, raise one eyebrow very high, glare steadily at him, walk slowly to his desk, and stand right beside him for a few minutes while you conduct your lesson. Before you leave his sweating side, whisper that he'd better behave or *else* (usually the principal's office or a telephone call home). Never stop your lesson for misbehavior if you can avoid it, but if stop it you must, take the time to do full justice to handling the episode. You won't regret it. Every so often a child—usually the one with lots of troubles or no home discipline—will tell horror stories about you, but most of the children will respect you and appreciate that you are aiding their learning by maintaining firm structure. Once an incident is over, forget it and go on teaching. (See the hilarious Jenny Gray books [Gray, 1974; 1968] for both organizational and discipline tips.)

9. Conditions for Success

THE TREATMENT OF learning disabilities is outside the child in the environment. If you wish to change the child's behavior so that he shows learning, you must make changes in those portions of his environment which are instructional. To see what works, you can change the organization of the classroom, at least as it applies to the learning-disabled pupil; you can change the kinds of instructions you give him; you can change the materials you use with him. The model for all this is programmed instruction.

Most of you have seen programmed materials and perhaps have used them yourselves. Essentially such materials break the task to be learned into tiny steps and force learning before the learner is able to proceed to the next step. Programmed instructional materials are nothing if not organized; they tell the learner precisely what to do and whether he has done it correctly at each step of the way. They differ from regular methods by thoroughly structuring the learning process for success. You must aim to do this in teaching the learning-disabled pupil. In both reading and arithmetic, the Distar programs do it (Engelmann and Bruner, 1969; also see Kost, 1972, for detailed descriptions of Distar use in the regular classroom).

CHARACTERISTICS OF THE CLASSROOM

For learning-disabled children, appropriate classroom structure is governed by the basic assumptions we have already discussed. The remedial target is selected and aim is taken. Anything in the classroom that can assist in taking aim should be used. Primarily, this means reducing distractions so that the child's attention and efforts are directed as nearly as possible at the goals you select and not elsewhere. The learning-disabled child's work area may need to be a table or desk isolated by a screen or bookcase from the other children. Many classrooms already have various centers where different activities proceed simultaneously, so one more will not be anything out of the ordinary. There is no need to buy an expensive learning booth, though there are people more than willing to sell them to you. Contact your local Sears or other appliance store for a cardboard refrigerator or washer-dryer combination box. Ask the pupil's parents, if they are do-it-yourself inclined, or a shop teacher to cut it so that it is three-sided. Paint the outside attractively, but leave the inside a solid, subdued color. The child sits inside at a desk and the whole affair is positioned so that the child cannot see or be seen by the others.

If yours is the older-fashioned classroom with all the desks facing one way and all the pupils on the same page at the same time (which of course they actually are *not*), revision of your set-up may be worth thinking about. A study carrel in one portion of your room for the learning-disabled child to use on his remedial work may arouse curiosity and envy among the other children, who will want one too. Many regular children speedily appreciate the advantages of the screened-off learning area and may press you for their own. In some rooms the study carrel is used as a reward and the pupils vie for it. After his installation in the carrel, you can check on the child from time to time as a natural part of your movement about the classroom. He will need frequent rewards and re-starting if his progress has been stalled. If you cannot provide a study carrel, you at least can face the child's desk or table to the wall or corner to reduce distractions. Make it clear to him and the others that this is not a punishment, but a help. The carrel is so much more preferable that we cannot recommend it highly enough. One or more study carrels should be standard equipment in every classroom.

If the learning-disabled child is not in his study carrel, he should be seated near your desk. You can guide him more effectively there on the work on which he is proficient and on his less disabled areas of learning disability. Too, you can give praise and attention more easily if the child is right under your nose. You can seize more opportunities to recognize the child and give him the special boosts helpful to building a good relationship. The better the relationship, the more the child may be willing to work for you.

Learning-disabled children like predictable routines. All too much of their lives will have been baffling, worrisome, and even alarming. Establish order and supportive structure for them throughout the day. At all times they should know what is coming next. Prepare them well beforehand for changes in routine so they know what to expect. Alternate quiet activities with group discussions or educational games. If scheduling permits, plan films and physical education late in the day since such activities tend to overstimulate the hyperactives, including the learning-disabled hyperactives.

Since attention span often is short, plan activities for short periods only. Permit frequent breaks, if necessary, but try to make these changes of pace rather than pure rest, though that will be needed too. Judging whether a break is truly needed will require your cunning. It is not as if this pupil is entirely a little wingless angel: he may not be above fudging, and who wouldn't after so much toil and maybe a history of grinding failure, shame, lectures at home and school, loss of privileges, and who knows what? Be firm, but take into consideration that the attention span of your learning-disabled pupil may be less than that of your average pupil.

CHARACTERISTICS OF INSTRUCTIONS

With learning-disabled children the object always is to aim directly for the target. This means assignments must be individualized, a point made a half dozen times above. Having floundered so much in the past, this pupil will appreciate your explicit statement of your expectations of him in terms of his remedial work. Tell him exactly what you expect him to do, exactly how to do it, exactly how he is to know he is doing it correctly, and exactly what will come after he is finished.

Remedial work follows a series of steps in organized sequence. As we have said, the model for teaching the learning-disabled is programmed instruction. Learning must take place before advancing. Where learning does not take place, the steps may need to be shortened or the pathway rerouted. Knowledge of success helps impel the taking of new steps. To avoid confusing the child, make instructions brief. Give only one worksheet or well structured lesson at a time. Do not give the pupil a blank page and tell him to write a letter, draw a picture, or do anything else without structure. Speak slowly and distinctly and be well organized. Try to be sure the child knows what you are talking about at each step before advancing to the next. Make every effort to maintain the child's attention and not let it waver. The more organized, concise, and specific you are, the better you will be able to do this. Lack of preparation on your part will be noticed by the pupil. Deadly little pauses while you hunt for this, fiddle with that, and apologize for this and that will cause your esteem to nose dive in the pupil's eyes and perhaps in yours too.

You may use any of the following techniques to catch and hold attention and to aid the pupil's memory:

Attention may be aided systematically by color-cues. The difficult letter or letter combination may consistently be traced over by you in some bright color. For example, the round part of *b* can be colored in red and the round part of *d* in blue. The first letter(s) of words can be colored in green and the last in red. The right-hand column in arithmetic problems can be bordered in green. Green is always the color-cue for where to start, and red is always the color-cue for where to stop. A bright ribbon can be tied to the wrist of the dominant hand to assist in learning the left-right distinction. You can underline in color important letters, numbers, operations, instructions, words, phrases, sentences.

You can use larger-than-usual print and fewer things per page to direct the pupil's attention. Magic markers can be used to border sections on a page of the pupil's material to help him keep his eyes within a given space or to compel him to follow a particular sequence. Likewise you can cover or fold

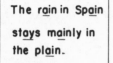

REPETITION

ISOLATION

SIZE

come

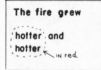

INTENSITY:
COLOR-CUE

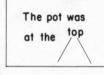

COLOR-CUE

POSITION

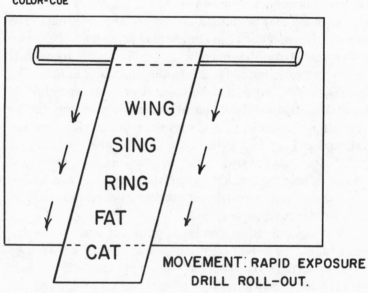

MOVEMENT: RAPID EXPOSURE
DRILL ROLL-OUT.

under a part of a page or even a word to direct the pupil's attention. Repetition and review are invaluable aids to attention and memory. Use them.

CHARACTERISTICS OF MATERIALS

A classroom can be organized to predispose the learning-disabled pupil to being able to learn. Instructions can be presented clearly to tip the predisposition further in the proper direction. Motivation can be created or maintained by various reward systems and praise. The final piece in the puzzle of finding means to the end is figuring out what materials to use. This topic brings us close to some of the honest-to-goodness particulars we suggest below in the various academic areas.

You will know only too well that the regular materials have not worked with the learning-disabled pupil. Here, as elsewhere, flogging a dead horse is a profitless task, but there is more than one way to skin a cat: different materials must be tried. If you are specifying targets and goals, if you are breaking the gap between as-is and the goal into steps, and if you are experimenting, the standard text almost certainly will not fit.

Fitting material is dictated by the pupil's instructional needs. You have to work out the exact fit, and the only way to know is by the result: has the pupil in fact begun to learn? If not, and if you can't think of some other reasonable explanation, that means the materials or the methods by which you present them need to be altered. If the alteration in a particular case is color-cuing the first letter of words green and the last red, is it materials or instructions you have changed? Many cases like that will be moot. It makes no difference: results are the name of the game.

As far as materials are concerned, several specific characteristics always will be found in those that work. For one thing, they are individualized. Materials also need to be concrete. Concrete materials are not just seen or heard; they may also instruct by being felt, moved, assembled, or otherwise handled. Counting discs, abacuses, Cuisenaire rods, number lines, dominoes, and alphabet blocks with raised letters are examples of concrete materials. If fitting materials are only seen or heard, most likely they will have glamour or otherwise be contrived to make their message unavoidable. For example, you might literally tape drawings of an apple for *a,* an elephant for *e,* and so on, to the pupil's desk to remind him of short vowels. Other concrete materials such as forcing-puzzles may be useful:

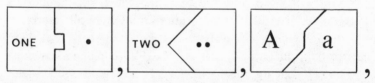

and so forth. Concrete materials often are fun and gamelike. Expensive ones can be ordered from catalogs. Inexpensive, maybe even free ones can be secured by showing the catalog to the pupil's parents or to a shop teacher in your local junior or senior high, pointing to the pictures of what you need, and telling the parents or teacher you know a way they can be of assistance. Be careful that you are not duplicating copyrighted or patented material, of course. You won't have to worry about this much. No one could patent wooden alphabet letters, for instance.

10. Reversals

REVERSALS ALWAYS APPLY to some specific instructional area, and we could deal with the subject entirely under the area headings of reading, writing, spelling, and arithmetic. But reversals are such a common learning disability that we have given the subject a section of its own. There is some repetition later. What we talk about here applies mainly to lower-case letters, which are much more reversible than upper case. With LD children you teach upper-case letters first (see Chapter Eleven). Probably that is best for all children.

First graders commonly reverse letters in their copying. As the months pass, so do reversals—for most children. Some few will be reversing in the second grade but most of them will say "Oops!" when you point out the errors and gradually self correct the reversal tendency. A very few, the learning-disabled, never seem to learn to watch their *p*'s and *q*'s no matter how many times you may point out the errors. They may reverse letters, parts of words, whole words, or numbers. On rare occasions—maybe once in ten years—you will find a genuine mirror-writer. For reversers, ranging from the mild to the severe, we have written this section.

The remedies for reversals depend on how severe the problem is. Use of the Jordan Left-Right Reversal Test (Jordan, 1973) can help determine the severity of the problem. For a child who reverses only a few letters in written spelling or copying, it may be sufficient just to say "Watch closely!" or "Look again!" as you sit by him following his work and spot a reversal. It may even be sufficient just to circle the reversed letter on papers you return to the child or do the circling while checking his work at his desk or yours. While the child reads aloud to you, stop him immediately at a reversal and ask him what he said, or you might ask him what the reversed word means in that context. He may notice the error as soon as you draw attention to it. This stopping technique is good with other reading errors too, so long as they are not very frequent. It may help the child develop the habit of re-reading when the meaning of a sentence sounds odd or makes no sense at all.

Somewhat tougher cases, and many of them will be, may demand that you color-cue the reversed letters in material from which the pupil is copying. For example, *m* could be done in yellow and *w* in blue. Naturally, you will call attention to why you are coloring the problem letters and ask the pupil to watch them very carefully. If words are being reversed, you can circle the first and last letters in green and red, respectively, or you can trace over the first and last letters in those colors. You can print reversed words with a bridge between the first letter or blend (we use the term blend for digraphs, diphthongs, and double letters) and the rest of the word. For example, w_as and s_aw.

For persistent or numerous reversals, more stringent measures are needed. A tracing–saying method is excellent for eliminating reversals along with other errors (Fernald, 1943). Print the word to be learned on a lined card in letters large enough that the pupil can trace the letters with his fore-finger and feel distinctive movements for the distinctive letters. After a number of repetitions he may say the word by syllables while tracing it if there is more than one syllable. Finally he says the whole word while doing the tracing. Repeat the procedure with the pupil doing the tracing with his pencil. Then have him print the word himself, first while looking at it and then *from memory*. If that hurdle is passed successfully, place the word in the child's own word bank. For the word bank you can use some type of little box, preferably of sturdy material, in which flash cards can be stored. The learned words are printed on separate cards.

In all tracing–saying, the learning may be more efficient if you put a weighted wristband on the child's dominant wrist. Kost (1972) advocates that the wristband be made by sewing two square lead drapery weights into a strip of red cotton three inches by nine inches. The slack is then taken up by a six-inch piece of elastic. This makes the wristband easy for the child to put on and remove. This kind of weighted wristband accentuates the distinctive feelings involved in making the various letters, and thus it promotes learning.

Other techniques for eliminating reversals can force strict left-to-right progression and attention to detail. Use graph paper and mark the left margin in green, because green is for going. In demonstrating left-to-right progression put letters in successive squares on the graph paper and number the squares left-to-right. Have the child reproduce your production in the squares below. Then have him copy words from a book onto the graph paper, numbering all the letters as he goes.

Another forced-attention, left-to-right technique requires the pupil to cover a word with a card and move it slowly to the right, thus exposing one letter at a time in a left-to-right progression. The same method may be used in reading an entire line of print. A variation on this card trick uses a window-slot card like this:

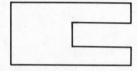

The slot is as high as a line of print, and the child moves the card from left to right, thereby preventing his looking back and causing him to watch each letter as it disappears under the card. The first of these two card tricks is helpful, but the latter is excellent in reducing regressions in reading (for those who read). To eliminate reversals, you may also use the window-slot card with the slot on the left:

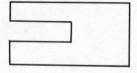

Another good forced-attention, left-to-right technique is having the child simply use his finger or pencil to point under each successive letter as he reads.

One of the best forced-attention, left-to-right methods for eliminating reversals is teaching the child to type. Availability and size of the typewriter play a part in whether you can use this method, but if there is a typewriter available and the child's hands can span the keyboard, teaching him to type can hardly be topped. It helps with letter identification too. The child should be trained right out of a standard typing manual and should not hunt and peck, which would entirely defeat your purpose. Two helpful guides for use with children are *You Learn to Type* (Lloyd and Krevolin, 1966) and *Young Fingers on a Typewriter* (Petitclerc, 1973). At the very least, typing will produce somewhat neater papers than would come from those who simply cannot overcome handwritten reversals and other writing disabilities. You will find that the typing does not especially distract the other children after the first few days. Ideally the typing child should have a typewriter at home as well as at school.

Reversal word games and flash cards can be helpful in eliminating reversals. Construct flash cards of the most frequently reversed words and use them in the regular way. Some words which can be used are: bag, bat, bin, bud, bus, but, cod, dad, den, dog, dot, gas, gum, Mac, mad, mid, nab, net, nod, on, pal, pan, Pam, pin, pit, ram, rap, rat, saw, tap, top, and tug. Show the child that by changing the first *d* in "dad" to *b* it becomes "bad." Ask him to form other words from a list of given words by changing the first letter.

11. Reading

READING IS THE most important skill learned in school. Everything else, eventually even arithmetic, depends upon it. Few learning-disabled children are disabled in every aspect of reading, but there are those who are. Usually there will be areas of relative strength and weakness. Once you have identified the deficits as precisely as you can, a variety of techniques may be used to produce reading skill where there was none or weakness before. The deficits or weaknesses always are instructional in nature, such as reversals, substitutions, and omissions, not such things as poor auditory-vocal sequencing. The remedial activities will aim for the instructional deficit, not for some hypothetical underlying whatnot.

In remedial reading for the learning-disabled, the most general principle is making certain each step in the sequence between as-is and the goal is thoroughly learned before advancing to the next step. You must aim your energy directly at the target in question. If, for example, the child cannot learn the short *a* sound, drop everything else until you have succeeded in teaching it to him. Do not overload the pupil's learning system. Distinctions among the short vowels often are enormously difficult for such a pupil to learn. You should not throw all the short vowels at him at once, but first teach one, then teach a second, then teach the distinction between the first and the second. It may take a long time to do this. Once this is done, you may advance to a third short vowel. This is just an illustration of the general principle and will be repeated later in more detail.

Learning disabilities in reading range from not recognizing the alphabet letters by shape (matching) to marked lack of sufficient comprehension relative to age, grade, intelligence, and word recognition level; we are talking about word-calling. For your purposes lack of ability to recognize letters by shape obviously is far more important than word-calling. The good word-caller may make it through school more or less on schedule if his spelling, writing, and arithmetic are halfway adequate, and go on not only to pass for normal in the everyday world, but to be normal. Hardly any ordinary adult reading requires skills above the fifth grade or newspaper level and few jobs do. Unless college is one of the expected performances of the word-caller, we may not need to worry about him much, and there are few of them anyhow. For those who do not learn to call letters by name, a different fate awaits. They may not even be going to the second grade until they have failed the first as many times as allowed in your school district. The severity of the learning disability is defined by how early it is generally noticeable in the child's work and by how pervasively it would affect his future career in school and out, were it to go uncorrected.

BUILDING FROM THE GROUND FLOOR

In what follows we begin with what is needed with the child who does not know the letters by shape and then move slowly in the direction of word-calling. You will need to take some learning-disabled children through this entire remediation section from *a* to *z*, while with others you do not have to start at the ground floor. Do make certain the ground floor is firm, though, before you begin at some higher level.

Matching by shape.

Some people think letter sounds should be taught first; we do not, because letter names are easier than letter sounds in the case of vowels and roughly the same in the case of consonants (Jenkins, Bausell, & Jenkins, 1972). Only the names of *h*, *q*, *w*, and *y* have little or no connection to their sounds.

Start at the simplest level. If a child does not know the alphabet letters by name, you first need to find out whether or not he can match letters by shape. That is, if you showed him an *A*, and said, "Find another one of those in this line," which consisted of *B*, *X*, *O*, *R*, *A*, could he indicate the *A*? If not, or if not consistently in a number of such matching problems, then you certainly know why he cannot *name* the letters, much less do anything so advanced as learn the sounds the letters make. Here you would have to go back all the way to the beginning if the game of results is ever to be won or even played. The tracing-saying technique, complete with wristband, described in the chapter on reversals is your best bet here. The pupil will be looking at, hearing you say, tracing with his finger, and saying himself the name of the letter. He then repeats the procedure using his pencil. This hits his brain from every angle. The letters must be printed on lined cards of fairly rough texture, and the letters must be large enough that finger-tracing and pencil-tracing give a definite feel for the distinctive shape and orientation of the letter. The letters must be printed, and naturally they must look like the print which will appear in the pupil's first reading material. Sadly, of course, most of those letters are lower case. However, for the disabled (we recommend it for everyone), the capital letters are easier to learn because they are more distinctive looking, more simply constructed (Fuller, 1974), less reversible, and bigger. Construct your own upper-case-only material, or get some from your curriculum supervisor. Renée Fuller's materials are one possibility (see references). The simple ability to tell letters apart may be the best predictor of future reading ability (Gibson, 1968; Luria, 1966; Satz and Friel, 1974).

Use upper case until knowledge of it is firmly established. There is no use arousing the child's contempt for logic by telling him right off that A is $\mathbf{a}$ is $\mathbf{Q}$ is $\mathbf{a}$. You must bide your time before springing this baffling, even outrageous piece of information on the child's immature mind, and then only bit by bit. Do not overload the learning system or else it will never be able to cope with the more maddening aspects of phonics.

At any event, establish identification, at least by shape, of upper-case letters first; you very well may have taught most of the letter names too by tracing-saying and probably will have. Your first aim, however, is matching. Can the pupil now find another A in a small group of letters? If so, solidify the knowledge and have some letter-finding fun by having the child circle all the *A*s on a page you have printed or typed. Have him go in a left-to-right direction always, and have him hold a straightedge under each line to prevent eye straying. You might need to use a card with a slot large enough to let only a few letters show, or you might need to have the child point to each successive letter while you say, "Is that an *A*?" for each one. This latter gets in a few more licks, if needed, for learning letter names. If the child has to look back at the most recently circled *A*, that is okay: *you are teaching, not testing*. Ultimately the *A* must be identified by mental image, however. Once he knows *A*, then advance to *B*, and once you reach *Z*, you will have taught matching. Few learning-disabled children will need this extreme measure, but some will. We have gone into such detail here to illustrate general learning-disabilities remediation procedure.

Letter naming.

After the child has learned matching, work can begin on his learning to call the upper-case letters by their names. The tracing-saying and letter-finding procedures probably will have taught him the names of most of the letters. If he identifies all but a few letters at this stage, your task and his will be ever so much easier than if most of their names still defy him. If, say, *B*, *D*, *H*, and *K* are the only ones he still cannot reliably name, go into intensive tracing-saying on *B*. Present *B* in common words; have the child find it in sentences. Then present *B* along with a well-established letter such as *O* again and again on flash cards. Repeat the procedure with *D*. Then begin to contrast *B* and *D* both with tracing-saying and flash ~ards. Point out how the two differ in looks and feel. Once the distinction is established, move on to the other troublesome

method does not succeed, we cannot be more
Something will work, but you and your school
will need to invent it together.

If tracing-saying and letter-finding for matching purposes
have not taught *any* letter names or only one or two, you have
on your hands a learning disability severe enough to be very
rare, assuming, of course, that the child is not actually mentally retarded. A learning disability of this nature goes beyond
the scope of this book. You and your school psychologist will
need to work together with a good deal of diligence to reach
any solution at all. A special class for such a child would be
more than warranted. With such a child it might be revealing
for you to experiment by pointing to a letter and asking yes-
or-no questions like "Is that an *A*?" You might find he does
know the names when he does not have to *say* the names. He
might be able to point to letters upon request or even print
them. Such a child will have an aphasia, presumably related
to a malfunction of some part of the brain, of which there are
various sorts. We ourselves cannot recall them and feel no
particular sense of deprivation, though the subject is fascinat-
ing. For those so minded, the subject may be pursued in Eisenberg (1964), Eisenson (1954), Ewing (1930), Johnson and
Myklebust (1967), or Van Riper (1972).

After upper-case identification comes lower-case identification, to pursue to the hilt the subject of the child who has
not learned letter names. This is relatively small potatoes since
so many lower-case letters have the good grace to be identical
in shape to their upper-case versions. All you may need to do
is teach the child to look at your alphabet wall chart when he
encounters a small letter he fails to recognize. You might tape
a small version of such a chart to his desk or inside his study
carrel. With recalcitrant cases, use flash cards. The upper and

lower cases are side by side; the child can name the lower case since he already knows the upper, but he sees both. Have him trace and say the lower-case letter some, and the letter-finding game can be indulged in again. Forcing puzzles are fun too,

as B\b , D⌐d , and so forth. The disaster

areas will generally be *b, d, p, q, n, u, m, w*. Color-cuing will be your chief relief there, with other tricks such as placing a picture of a boy to the pupil's right since the round part of the *b* is on the right, and a picture of a dog to the pupil's left, since the round part of the *d* is on the left. Tactics like that should establish the lower-case letters.

Mental images and mental sounds.

We mentioned "mental images" above and how letters must be established mentally in matching rather than the pupil always looking back at previous examples. When you write you never or only rarely have to think what a letter looks like before you write it. The whole process is nearly automatic. Your hand is writing and you are thinking what to put into writing, not about what each letter looks like. (At least those have this privilege whose hands are not in the fierce grip of a standard penmanship manual!) This skill is learned, and if you watch the concentrated frowns and protruding tongues of first and second graders, you will be vividly reminded how laborious that learning might have been for you. When the skill is automatic, the mental image part has long since been bypassed, but it was there at an initial stage. The young writer, or printer, first recognizes that he must print a certain letter. Then he may consider what that letter looks like. If this consideration is productive, he then puts it down on paper. With the passage of time and the piling up of experience, the intermediary step becomes shorter. Making the letter eventually becomes automatic.

Visual images are more important than mental sounds in writing since no one ever heard the shape of a letter. But what if you are writing automatically and need to write a word you recognize you cannot spell? Before resorting to the dictionary or your neighbor, you may do one of two things which are not strictly separable: spell the word to yourself and consider the sound of it, or write it tentatively and look at your production with a critical eye. We agree that the looking is the more important, but clearly the hearing enters in, and in some people as much as the visual. There is thus more than one intermediary step between recognizing the need for a letter and producing it. The child almost certainly will hear the name of the letter too. The fact of the matter is that he quite likely will hear the letter he needs, summon up the visual image, and then write it down. However, he did first have to learn to attach the name (a sound) to the printed letter (a visual shape).

We are not trying to drive you to distraction with a chicken-or-egg riddle. We are trying to illustrate how complex the stages are in learning something as automatic as writing. And by so illustrating, you get a feel for the variety of ways and levels at which a learning disability may make itself felt, all of which have implications for remediation. With most children, visual matching of shapes is first, then names (sounds) are attached to the shapes. By then, knowledge of how to move the muscles to produce the shapes on paper is being acquired, possibly by tracing-saying. The mental sounds and mental images of the letters have varying degrees of importance at various stages of the process. Finally, with the mental images having been the more important intermediary step, the whole business becomes automatic in the regular child, but maybe not so in the learning-disabled.

Some learning-disabled children have a hard time thinking what a letter looks like, just as some have a hard time matching or attaching names to letter shapes. This impedes spelling and printing, and you might notice the concentrated frowns and protruding tongues here too. You can work on the mental images with letter (or number) memory games. Show the child a letter, remove it for a second or two, and ask him to reproduce it. Do this for all the letters and gradually increase the length of time between exposure and when you say, "Now write it." This can be a diagnostic game in class. Those children who cannot succeed at it, and if they are giving other evidence of learning disability, must be helped individually by you or someone else. When your class plays the game as a group, you will soon know the importance of the child's hearing the letter, because so many of them will say the letter aloud (and may be promptly shushed by others). Those who have to say the letter aloud should be allowed to; the visual image is not automatic in them yet. In individualized remedial work, let them say the letters as long as they need to, but the automatic visual level will probably be reached eventually. If it never is, a little whispering never hurt anyone. Many of us adults read entirely at the hearing level, having never moved from sight to comprehension without the hearing step. We daresay actual lip movements occur in some people. This is no big deal, though it keeps the speed-reading folks in the money.

The group game in the paragraph above can be played in the other direction too. You call out the sound, and the children write down the letter. If you are devoted to traditional phonics, this is a good game. Undeniably it can be played well by children who are already proficient in traditional phonics; it helps them in spelling phonetic words not encountered before. Realistically, though, how often in real life, aside from spelling bees, do we have to spell phonetic, or for that matter, nonphonetic words we have not encountered before? We recommend a different approach to phonics below.

Phonics.

Phonics waxes and wanes in popularity. The topic is always good for a lively discussion, not to say a donnybrook, in a teachers' lounge or school board meeting. Current thinking is that the learning-disabled, if they are "strong in the visual modality" and "weak in the auditory modality," should not have phonics. We believe this view to be a gross simplification, though it is not entirely without merit. There is simply no way to avoid the fact that sounds *must* be attached to letter shapes if one is to learn to read (Gillingham and Stillman, 1960).

The ease with which sounds are attached to letter groups varies widely in the English language. "The" could never be taught by phonics, so it is taught by the sight, whole word, or look-say method. Attempted phonetically, "the" might come out tuh-huh-ee. Yet many words can best be attacked through traditional phonics by syllable, such as superman, or by single letter, such as big. In all cases the final product is the attachment of sounds to letter shapes. Thus we believe everyone who reads with his eyes learns to read by phonics. So in fact do braille readers since they attach sounds to patterns of shapes, too. If the learning-disabled child is "weak in the auditory modality," he is going to be learning to read by phonics just like everybody else, though perhaps not so speedily.

Since most children do learn traditional phonics readily,

we advise that it be your way of teaching reading to beginners. This brings up the matter of what kind of phonics to use since there are some children, among them almost invariably the learning-disabled, who do not take to traditional phonics. We recommend Speech-to-Print Phonics (Durrell and Murphy, 1972). This ingenious system is excellent for the learning-disabled pupil who is past matching and who has the stumbling beginnings of reading ability; however, it does teach everything down to the level of letter-naming, if necessary. It can be used in groups or individually, by you, your aide, a supervised tutor or parent. It can be used with your whole class right from the first day in teaching reading. Most importantly, from our view, it dispenses with agonized sounding out and teaches reading as well as phonics, so by our definition it is genuinely instructional. The learning-disabled pupil will need more than this phonics, but he will be benefited by it almost certainly.

Some teachers post elaborate phonics charts which give perhaps a dozen phonics rules, all of them with exceptions appearing in some of the very earliest words learned and prove no rule other than that traditional phonics is fraught with booby traps. We feel that use of a dictionary is better when a child realizes he cannot pronounce a word, provided he can use a dictionary. It is faster and surer than checking back and forth between the wall chart and the word in question whose pronunciation quite possibly will not be governed by any of the rules in any case. When working with a learning-disabled child individually on oral reading, tell him right away the pronunciation of any word on which he pauses or, worse, on which he begins tortured and tedious sounding out.

We very much like the Initial Teaching Alphabet (Downing, 1964) which does something very commonsensical. With some additions and subtractions, the ITA makes our alphabet, and thus spelling and reading, almost entirely phonetic. It was invented for beginning readers and has had some success, but of course the children eventually had to go on to the regular alphabet because that's the way of the real world. We wish the real world could be changed and think it should be. We believe the ITA or something like it should be the standard, permanent form of the English language for everybody. We advocate that curriculum specialists and those in the world of publishing give serious thought to phasing ITA into texts and print, year by year, so that eventually everyone can read it (O'Halloran, 1973). Then a complete changeover could be effected. However appealing this may be to think about, the ITA may never be adopted. We do not advocate its use now for the learning-disabled pupil since he will have to revert to regular language eventually.

Auditory Discrimination.

We admit to a psychologese term here, though you need not regard it with the deepest misgivings. Auditory discrimination is simply the skill with which one can tell apart similar but different sounds which one can hear perfectly well. If the sounds of *p* and *b* register loud and clear but do not register as different in the child's mind, some of what you say to him will not make sense and spelling certain words will be impossible. Phonics will be a chore too, and since we confidently assert that all reading is phonetic if not always traditional sounding-out (see above), we must address auditory discrimination. Problems in it will often be noticed from the child's speech. If he makes certain sounds alike which should be different, perhaps he can't tell them apart. If you suspect an auditory discrimination problem, mention it to your school psychologist, and he or she most likely will administer some kind of test for it.

Remediation of auditory discrimination problems is difficult to fit into our practical approach to learning-disability remediation. In that approach, you will recall, remedial tasks must be clearly pertinent and related to regular instructional tasks. They must not be the out-moded methods of learning lists of nonsense words, walking beams, tracing mazes, and the like. We will dispense with apologies and simply admit we can't fit auditory discrimination into the practical approach well enough to waste space here trying to do so. There is a commercially available program which makes remediation of auditory discrimination problems fun to work on (Lindamood and Lindamood, 1971). As mentioned in Chapter Three, recent evidence has suggested that auditory discrimination may have far less connection with reading ability than previously thought (Hammill and Larsen, 1974), so we may not need to get ourselves really wrought up over it except in severe cases.

For remediation, if you do not use the Lindamood and Lindamood program, or some other, the school psychologist most likely will devise a procedure by which you or a helper calls out pairs of similar-sounding words incorporating the confused sounds identified by the test. The child must say whether the words are the "same" or "different." With younger children, these concepts may not be too well established and you may have to work on that first. To do this, start with pairs of words that are blatantly the same or different, as "elephant, elephant" and "boy, girl." Keep working on such pairs until the child has arrived at the concepts of same and different. You will be surprised at how difficult this will be for some children, so be patient. The commercially available program is better than what you and your school psychologist will be able to work out unless time galore is spent on the matter, so you might look into it. Speech-to-Print Phonics helps with auditory discrimination also.

Once you get to auditory discrimination proper, zero in on the pairs of words so they are closer and closer to being identical. Of course you will have pairs of identical words embedded in your lists so that the child can say "same" sometimes. You may have to start with the severely disabled child watching you, and you may need to make exaggerated lip movements and sounds. Your aim is for him to be able to distinguish the sounds with his back turned and your pronouncing in a normal speaking voice. A version of this can be done as a group game in which you write one key word on the chalkboard and have each child pronounce it. Then you read a list of words and the children clap once whenever they hear a word with the same beginning sound as the one on the board. This can be used for ending sounds too. Happily, increasing maturity and ability to guess words from context seem to produce a diminution of auditory discrimination problems. The remedies suggested should be persistently tried, however, for the more rapidly the problem is surmounted, the more likely the child is to profit from your teaching.

A Recap and More Tips on How to Firm Up the Foundation

So far in this section on reading—the most important academic skill—we have delved into matching by shape, letter-naming, mental images and mental sounds, phonics, and auditory discrimination. We have sought always to suggest workable remedial procedures which fit into regular instruction recognizably. We have sought to show that targets must be specified, goals set, brief steps taken between pupil as-is and the goal, and an experimental frame of mind kept. All this we have done fairly well except in auditory discrimination problems. We couldn't make that kind of remediation very instructional in terms of ordinary classroom activities, but we did suggest a program to make it fun. We will now lay out a distilled version of the practical approach to learning-disabilities remediation applied to reading problems. Later we will discuss specific uses of the method with pupils who can read well enough to have omissions, substitutions, and so forth—the kinds of reading errors we traditionally think of in regard to remedial reading.

We stated above that the most general principle of practical remedial reading for the learning-disabled is that you must make certain each step between pupil as-is and the goal is learned thoroughly before advancing to the next step. When a difficulty arises in achieving one of those steps, you first must simplify and concentrate on the difficult area. Eliminate everything from consideration but the problem step, and direct all your effort and cunning to overcoming it. If you still fail, gracefully move to something easier and return after you have devised a different way of approaching the matter.

Each step of a sequence must become automatic for the pupil. If he is stumbling about and you are throwing too many things at him at once, his learning system is overloaded. He may even forget or fumble on steps which previously were established securely. This is one reason we discourage laborious sounding out and favor the Speech-to-Print Phonics system which dispenses with it. Agonized sounding out is awfully frustrating to the child and may bring out hair-tearing tendencies in you. Also it gives the child actual practice in incorrect responses. Whenever the child is allowed to get by with some mistake, he may be thinking that something incorrect is correct. That is bad to think even for a moment. Likewise, if a child hesitates more than a few seconds over a word, say it for him. A long delay naturally means the item to be learned is not yet automatic. It amounts to an error of sorts since it allows the mental practice of incorrect responses. The child must have a solid correct footing at all times.

You should plan the remedial material and judge the length of the learning steps on the basis of the pupil's performance. *He should be correct at least eight or nine times out of ten* or he will be too frustrated to learn enjoyably and keep his feeling of hope kindled. Success breeds motivation. If there are too many errors, you must shorten the learning steps and take more precise aim. Excessive errors snowball because they demoralize the child and send his attention out the window. Furthermore, if the child makes several errors, you may, in a moment of laxity, let one go by, thus reinforcing an error.

For a step to become automatic, it must start out very simply. We have illustrated this amply in our sections on matching by shape and letter-naming. To become automatic a step must be practiced so thoroughly as to become overlearned. Do not stop when the child finally attaches the correct name to *b* once. Have him do so repeatedly until there is overlearning. Then and only then is it time to move on to the next step. Review those steps already taken from time to time, and don't wait long to do so.

When two bits of material to be learned cannot be distinguished by the child, as, say, if he simply cannot discriminate between short *a* and short *e*, you should do this: first concentrate on short *a* and use every means at your command to have it become automatic. For example, distinguish between short *a* and long *a* by reading pairs of words and having the child respond with "short" versus "long." This will be similar to auditory discrimination exercises. Then do the same for short *e*. Then review short *a* briefly. Then begin to contrast short *a* and short *e* in words where all the other elements are identical, as in "sat" and "set." You may have to use nonsense words, but that is all right as long as you tell the child they are not real words and why you are using them. Establish the distinction securely with the first two-word set, then move on to other such pairs whose only difference is the short vowel. Then gradually move on to words containing other different elements besides the short *a* and the short *e*. This makes the discrimination more and more secure. A good program for teaching short vowels is offered in the Merrill Linguistic Readers (Fries, Fries, Wilson, & Rudolph, 1966).

Building discriminations can be aided by using crutches and cues, as mentioned earlier. In the case of short vowels, which is the greatest area of trauma in phonics, the learning-disabled pupil may pronounce any short vowel with any other short vowel sound, rarely giving the long vowel sound for it. You can tape to his desk a little chart with a picture of an apple with *a*, an elephant with *e*, an igloo with *i*, an octopus with *o*, and an umbrella with *u*. You could and should put such a chart up for all the children, but the learning-disabled pupil will more likely look at the chart if it is actually taped to his desk or inside his study carrel. These picture-letter combinations stimulate learning correct pronunciations. When the child no longer needs them, he will stop looking at them.

Color-cuing is excellent in reading remediation, and it helps if you are fairly consistent in your use of colors. Green is always at the beginning and may be a single letter or a blend. In reading it will be on the left, and in vertical arithmetic problems it will be on the right. Red should represent the last sound in a word. Medial short vowels can be colored in yellow and long vowels in brown. We do not mean to encourage laborious sounding out by causing the pupil to look at, say, a four-color word. We simply suggest color-cuing as a way of drawing attention to distinctions. Consistent use of the same color for the same distinction is only reasonable.

Circling and underlining games are helpful in teaching attention to details which distinguish words one from the other.

cat	door	was	saw
can	drop	went	sam
car	dune	was	was
cat	door	man	wax
cab	boon	saw	saw

Tell the children to find a word just like the word on top above the line in each column, and to circle it.
Or:

mat	met
bird	heard
door	sore
grow	great
walking	playing

Tell the children to circle the parts which sound alike and underline the parts which sound different.

Review.

Learning-disabled children are notorious for learning a modest task after fierce effort on everybody's part, only to draw a complete blank or nearly so just minutes later when asked again. *There must be frequent reviews of the basic problem areas even after they seem well established.* Let us say you have finally taught the child the correct sound for a troublesome short vowel. You have then done so for a second troublesome short vowel. You have reviewed both vowels and then have succeeded in building up the distinction between the two. You have used word pairs where the vowel is the only difference and have moved slowly to words which require more careful looking. You have used various techniques of color-cuing and same-different games. At this stage your job on those vowels is not fully accomplished. You must review the whole business periodically. There should be several brief reviews during the very practice session in which you worked on the distinction. The next practice session should *begin* with a review. Do not begin it with a test. The child may have forgotten half of what you thought he had down pat, so do not discourage him with a full-scale test where he can see his failure. Instead, the test should be a brief review. You will be able to tell how automatic his responses are. By the third session, he may remember three-fourths of what was learned in the first session, and in the fourth session, his performance may be nearly perfect. Teach, don't test, until you are positive the child really can perform the task automatically.

Try to give variety to the reviews so that, for example, the child is not finding the word "cot" in the group "cat, cot, cut" with "cot" always in second position. That is to say, sheer rote performance of this kind of review may suggest perfect knowledge when the foundation has begun to erode. *Reviews should involve actual reading as soon as possible.* (Fuller's program [1974] actually has children reading after they know only four or five alphabet letters.) Naturally this should require only those skills the child already possesses since you won't want to produce fumbling. Tell the child why you are reviewing. Many of them gripe about baby stuff and the like. Tell the child his basic skill in his trouble area must be strong enough to keep him from getting confused, so that he can eventually learn to read like the other children. That should make the point. Retention and motivation may be increased when the learner knows why he must study. This is another argument for practical remediation rather than esoteric remediation: the child sees practical work as connected with his problem.

Traditional Reading Problems and Practical Remedies

We will now discuss the pupil who has become proficient enough in reading to be limited by traditional kinds of reading errors. Maybe remediation of the more basic reading disabilities such as matching by shape and so forth got him up to this level. Much more likely, he got this far on his own with regular instruction. The limitation may not come to light clearly until the child is stumbling around after he matches, letter-names, has some phonics skills, but then doesn't get much further. We are talking about errors such as regressions, omissions, and the like. We will briefly address each of them.

Regressions and repetitions.

These problems stem from faulty eye movements or from habitual insecurity and fear of words to come. Where there are eye-movement regressions, use straightedges and cards with window-slots, as suggested above. These forcing devices guide attention and mechanically prevent the child from regression in his eye movements (Heckelman, 1974). If he is repeating what he cannot see, that is, if you have moved the card left to right covering a word and he repeats the word, he is repeating from memory. Usually, though, he will be repeating because he has looked back; a window-slot card (with the slot on the right side) will prevent it until a new habit is established. When habitual insecurity seems the cause of regression, concert reading of easy passages with a model reader is a good remedy. Tape recording the child's reading and letting him play it back while he rereads the material is a good technique for drawing attention to repetitions. Sometimes that alone is enough to eliminate mild repetition habits or those repetition habits which have lived on even after the child has ceased to fear reading.

Omissions of words or parts of words.

Omissions are intriguing to consider. In silent reading who is to say whether a word has been omitted? It makes no difference if comprehension is adequate. Very good readers may omit a substantial proportion of words in light material when they read fast. Not a great deal of reading aloud goes on in real life anyhow. School children and teachers, news broadcasters, the President, and lecturers do most of it. The chief cure for the President, broadcasters, and lecturers is rehearsal, but that luxury does not apply to everyday classroom oral reading unless the child is fortunate enough to be able to count ahead to find out which paragraph he will be reading when his turn comes—a procedure you will fiendishly defeat, however, by skipping around. In the usual classroom situation the chief remedy for omissions is reducing the rate of reading. You may also sit next to the child and say, "Miss!" the instant an omission occurs. Do not be too emphatic in doing this; you don't want to cause regressions by stimulating insecurity. Concert reading and tape-recorded playback of his own reading are helpful to the child in reducing omissions. Left-side window-slot cards work well here too.

Substitutions of words.

Substitutions by the child can be most perplexing to you since so often the substitutions make no particular sense. This is another error which can only be detected in oral reading, but it has diagnostic importance. Typically it means the reading material is too hard. Substitution of words will go along with low comprehension; whenever comprehension is not in the 80–90 percent range, the material is not suitable for instructional purposes. The chief remedies are two: go back to easier material and work on building vocabulary. Since concert reading and tape-recorded playback only apply to easy material which is not read smoothly, they do not work here very well; if the material were easy, there probably would be few substitutions. If comprehension is high and substitutions occur, you could use concert reading and playback, or you could more economically ignore the whole matter if the substitutions are not too numerous.

Additions of words and parts of words.

Addition of words is another type of error noticed mostly in oral reading, though it can occur in copying. Like most of the traditional errors, it can be ignored if comprehension is high and the additions are not too numerous. Where it is a real problem, you can sit with the child and say, "Addition!" or "Extra!" the moment one occurs while he is reading, and this may help build attention to detail. You can use window-slot cards with the window in the center of the card,

to keep the child's eyes riveted to the word elements as the window-slot card is moved left to right. Concert reading can help this difficulty, as can tape-recorded playback, if the child is watching his material closely during the playback. *Emphasis should be on good phrasing, expression, and accuracy in oral reading, not speed;* this should reduce the number of additions.

Reversals.

The section on reversals above contained what you need to remedy reversals of letters (*p* and *q*, *b* and *d*, and so on). Briefly, we advocate the tracing-saying method to establish first one and then the other letter well so they can be letter-named correctly using flash cards. Then use letter-finding games in which all of one particular letter on a page are circled in one color by the child and all of the other letters are then circled in another color. In oral reading, stop the child instantly with "Reversed!" or "Backwards!" when you hear an incorrect pronunciation suggesting a reversed mental image or mental sound on the child's part. On your part this requires good auditory discrimination and good acoustics in the room in which you work. Window-slot cards are helpful too in forcing attention. Concert reading and tape-recorded playback are helpful also. Where a letter is reversed which is not, when reversed, like some other letter (*b* and *d* reversed look like each other, but a reversed *c* doesn't look like anything), see the general chapter on reversals. All these techniques should help the child watch his *p*'s and *q*'s.

Where reversals of words and phrases take place, use the finger-pointing technique in which the child leads his eyes with his finger under each successive word. Never discourage use of the finger in this way. If certain words or phrases are frequently reversed, tracing-saying is excellent, followed up by having the child write the word or phrase from memory repeatedly. Of course we do not mean the age-old "write 500 times, 'I will not . . . ' " punishment, which merely instills deep dislike for writing and academics. Any punishment which involves giving extra academic work backfires. Never, never do it. We mean five or six times with your emphasizing to the child that the repetition is needed to print the correct response on his brain. Lavish praise on him when he does it correctly and review often.

Word-calling.

Some very few children have an unusual ability to pronounce words correctly without the least idea what the words mean. If the older word-caller can comprehend at, say, the fifth-grade level, is semi-adequate in spelling, arithmetic, and so forth, the problem really makes no difference unless he is supposed by someone to be bound for college or some other training where actual high-level comprehension of the written word may be required. If that kind of word-caller has good intelligence, the remedy lies in asking him comprehension questions. You might do it sentence by sentence, and begin with material which the word-caller can comprehend at the 80–90 percent level, which will be well below his highest word-calling level. Ask him to express the same thought in different words. Give as many hints and as much aid as necessary. Remember, you are teaching, not testing. An extensive list of the low-vocabulary, high-interest books which word-callers are likely to comprehend is provided by Hiskey (1969). These books are also invaluable for reluctant readers and underachievers who are not learning-disabled in reading in upper grades of school. No school district should be without several series of low-vocabulary, high-interest books. To become a good reader any child, learning-disabled or not, must do lots and lots of reading. This point cannot be overemphasized, and the children will do much more reading if you provide them with interesting books. A general formula has been offered by Bond and Clymer (Della-Piana, 1968) for estimating a pupil's potential reading comprehension level: reading expectancy = [years in school $\times$ (IQ/100)] + 1. Other formulas have been developed also (Bruininks, Glaman, & Clark, 1973).

12. The Written Product in Language

THERE ARE TWO sorts of products in written language. They are writing and spelling. All writing is written, and so is most spelling. Some spelling is oral, and though not a great deal of this goes on in real life, it has its place in the early school years since it helps establish correct sequence of mental images and sounds which the child may transfer onto paper. Having a child repeatedly spell a word aloud, eventually without looking at its written form, is the way to drill on oral spelling or mental sounds. If a child is much worse in oral spelling than in written, and if the latter is at an acceptable level or nearly so, for practical purposes there is no problem unless someone has a fixation on spelling bees. If a child is much better in oral spelling than in written, then there is a problem worthy of remediation. The remediation has more to do with writing than with spelling.

To spell correctly, the child must correctly match a series of letters with an orally presented word or with an internal mental image or mental sound of the word. There can be no spelling unless the child has learned the mental images and mental sounds of the letters. Letter-naming is thus a predecessor to both oral and written spelling since it attaches the letter names to their visual symbols (Helms, 1967). When you say, "Write a *b*," the child is actually spelling that letter when he writes it.

Mental images and mental sounds not only are necessary for acquiring the ability to spell, but they are also necessary for acquiring the ability to write. True writing (not copying) is the translation of mental images and sounds into regulation shapes on paper, and in true writing the muscle-learning becomes largely automatic. There will be no writing or written spelling without the muscle-learning. Correct muscle-learning depends on considerable written practice in correct matching by shape, and, at the initial copying level, the child's vision steers his muscle-movements.

You can see that writing and spelling are closely related if you try to figure out which is the more basic and what has to be learned first. In most children all of this takes place more or less simultaneously, but we aren't worrying about most children, only the learning-disabled ones. With them, for all intents and purposes, you will not need to determine which comes first either, except to specify the child's disability initially. The rough logical sequence is matching by shape, letter-naming, muscle-learning (at first copying or tracing and then more automatic movements), mental images and sounds, and attachment of the muscle-learning to mental images and sounds. At the most advanced stage all this gets to be genuine writing and spelling. Writing–spelling follows roughly the sequence of stages in reading, except that muscle-movement in the hand is needed for writing and written spelling but not in reading. Some children learn to make the correct muscle-movements more easily than they learn the names of the written products of muscle-movements. The name may come to the child after he makes the muscle-movements.

Remediation of writing and spelling learning disabilities follows the remediation of reading problems up to a point. When you specify the target, you may find writing–spelling difficulties in matching by shape, letter-naming, mental images and sounds, and in phonics. In many instances the difficulty will be at some level of those skills which also contribute to learning to read. We can do no better than refer you to the previous sections on matching by shape and so on. Additionally, though, you may find the trouble in the manual muscle-learning which is peculiar to writing–spelling and is not part of reading, which has mouth muscle-learning. Many learning-disabled children finally begin to read though their writing and spelling remain atrocious. We have some practical remedial suggestions for writing–spelling disabilities, but there is an important point to make first. The basic academic objective of early education is teaching the child to read. If you could teach only one skill, this is the one you should choose. If nothing works in remedying the writing or spelling disabilities, but the child begins to read, don't nitpick. Consider both of you lucky that the student can comprehend the written word.

WRITING

Several distinctive muscle-movements must be learned before writing, whether in print or cursive, can be expected. The pupil must know how to hold the pencil. Watch the position of his elbow and forearm and wrist. Notice where his hand rests on the desk. We are convinced that many writing problems stem from improper positions of the arm, hand, and fingers (Kahn, 1970). We believe left-handed children in particular tend towards poor handwriting because they learn basic writing positions incorrectly. In a right-handed world it is difficult to show left-handed beginning writers how to hold the pencil because most teachers are right-handed themselves. Basically, the left-handed child should do everything in writing just the same as the other children, except that the position is a mirror-image. Above all, he should not be allowed to curl his hand around grotesquely, a condition arising from his natural desire to see and be guided by what he has already written. By positioning his hand and arm and paper in a mirror-image of the right-handed writer, the left-handed child will be able to see most of what he writes. His writing will look better than if the hideously curled position is allowed to develop. Don't let it develop. Once it is present, a remedial bulldozer is needed to root it out. You will have to reteach the movements involved in making all the letters and remain on constant guard against a recurrence of curling. An illustrated manual and a set of exercises for teaching left-handed children to write well has been developed by Plunkett (1967).

After the child, right- or left-handed, knows how to hold his arm, hand, fingers, pencil, and paper, there are some basic movements to learn (Arena, 1970). Have him perfect vertical, then horizontal, then diagonal lines, and finally loops:

$$| , — , / , \setminus , \times , \; \textit{llllllllll} \; .$$

The curl of the loops should be to the left or counterclockwise, because that is the way cursive writing loops loop when they are on the line (as in $\textit{l}$) or above it (as in $\textit{l}$). $\textit{rrrr}$

may be used, too, curling clockwise since most lower-loop letters do so. It might be best to stick with the counterclockwise loops at first. Most of the movements for letters will be taken care of by these practices.

It is time to get to the alphabet. You will have noticed that little children have no great regard for the distinction between lower case and upper case. They print big, and even if you try to drill in the importance of a capital letter at the beginning of a sentence or proper name, you will often find no great difference, if any, among the letters in size. More likely, the sizes will vary more or less at random. We advocate that you not try to teach upper and lower case simultaneously. Begin with upper case if you teach printing first (and most of you will) and lower case if you teach cursive first. Once upper case in printing is established, teach the rules for using lower case and then teach the necessary lower-case letters.

Teaching upper case in printing is much the same as teaching matching by shape and letter-naming. The tracing–saying method works well for those whose progress is slow enough to suggest learning disability in muscle-learning. Teach the letters one by one. Usually the child will want to learn to print his name first, and he may already be able to do it. If he can, review it and make sure the muscle-movements are correct. If they are not, reteach them. Particularly when you reach lower case, watch for "bottom starting" like a hawk: If the child is named Bobby and his lower-case *b*'s begin where a *6* stops, or if he's Billy and his *l*'s begin at the bottom and go up, swoop down on those awkward habits immediately and establish the proper ones. There are problems in doing this with a few letters, such as upper-case *M*. Obviously it is much more sensible to start at the bottom, jump up, down, up, down, than to have four separate paper-touchings by beginning each straight line at the top. Yet, to do the sensible thing with *A*, *M*, and *N* as capitals may invite bottom starting on other letters. It is probably better to begin all straight line movements at the top. In time, the child will economize on his own when he knows the letters well enough. If you are unsure just what the sequence of movements is in any letters, look on the back of the cover of an elementary tablet. Many tablets have illustrations of the letters with numbered arrows showing the direction and sequence of the movements comprising the various letters.

Print the first upper-case letter to be learned on a large card or sheet of paper. Slightly coarse-grained paper is desirable if you can find it for it accentuates the "feel" of the letters. We are not talking about sandpaper; if you use that you're going to produce very smooth, hot, perhaps even raw little fingertips! The paper must be lined in just the way the child's primary tablet is lined. To use unlined paper is to ask for jumbled letters. Have the child repeatedly trace the letter with his forefinger while saying the letter name. Naturally, in tracing the letter he will be making the movements in the same direction and sequence used in printing the letter. That is, his finger will be moving counterclockwise for *O*, starting at the top for *O* and *L*, and so forth. Once the movement practice has become well learned, guide the child in making the same movements with his pencil, and then let him do it by himself repeatedly. Eventually the child will be making the letter by himself from memory. Follow the same procedure for the other upper-case letters.

You then move on to lower case, which is now relatively easier than it would have been had you begun it before upper case. Wall and desk charts of lower- and upper-case pairs may be all that are needed once you instill the rule about the first letter of sentences and of proper names. Blessedly, not too many of the lower-case letters differ radically from their upper-case counterparts, with *a, b, d, e, f, g, h, q,* and *r* being the offenders. Tracing-saying and forcing puzzles such as

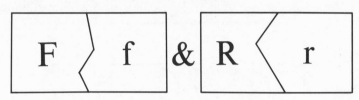

are useful on recalcitrant cases, but mostly you can count on osmosis to do the trick if you have a wall or desk chart available for the pupil to look at and if you can teach him to recognize when he needs to look at it.

As mentioned above, two lower-case letters are a bit of a trial since their normal form in book print is not like their usual form in children's guides to printing. They are *a* and *g.* The child will just have to cope here by your use of tracing–saying on both forms of both letters. Flash cards with *a* and *ɑ̀* and *g* and *ɡ* can be used too.

Jumbled letters were mentioned above. By this we mean letters that wobble from one to the next, vary in size, and otherwise fail to conform to standards. Jumbled letters include reversals which we have previously dealt with (see Chapter Ten). There is a good way to help remedy jumbled letters: use graph paper. The squares must be large enough for the small child's large print. One letter in each square works wonders for spacing. The vertical and horizontal lines forming each square's sides are an anchor and guide in letter formation since learning-disabled children are usually quite lost on blank paper.

An invaluable tool for forcing attention in printing and

later in cursive writing is the color-cued tablet. A tablet with the top lines shaded in one distinctive pastel color and the bottom lines in another distinctive pastel color, and divided by a solid black line, is helpful in teaching how far the on-the-line letters go: *a, c, e, i, m, n, o, r, s, u, v, w, x, z.* For example,

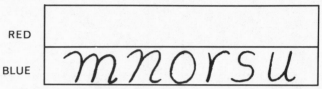

You might help the learning-disabled child further by providing vertical lines forming squares as with graph paper. Tablets with top and bottom lines in different colors but with a middle dotted line in black are good for tall letters and those with tails: *b, d, f, h, k, l, t; g, j, p, q, y.* For example:

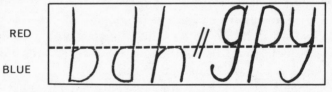

Surprisingly enough, learning-disabled children usually can write in cursive less disastrously than print. The reason is that with cursive, letters flow into each other, while in printing they start "in space" and thus have more chance for wobbling off course. We believe that children could be taught cursive from the start. It may come as a surprise to our younger readers, but a generation or so ago it was done that way in much of America. Printing, or manuscript as it has come to be called lately, emerged strongly later and now is ballyhooed as a prerequisite for cursive. Practically the only printing going on in adult life is done by teachers or sign painters on the job. Admittedly, knowing how to print the individual letters may help the pupil in letter-naming, but why must he continue to print? Use paper with widely spaced, clearly defined lines, and children will be able to write in cursive long before you ever imagined they could. Whenever you force printing on a child who is trying to write in cursive, you cramp his style. How many of you have said, "Wait till next year," to the child trying to write in cursive? Let him do it as soon as he wants. If you let him, you will soon be hearing praise from the parents: "Why, in Johnny's class, they're already using cursive!"

A word is in order about penmanship, by which we mean "pretty" writing in cursive. We have no fondness for the subject and feel far too much time can be devoted to it in grammar school. No educated person who handwrites a great deal follows what penmanship manuals say except grammar school teachers, and that is only because you have been subjected to incessant penmanship propaganda and practice for years. Do not stress penmanship. When the writing is legible it is a waste of time because it hinders thought processes in those who have to think how to write pretty. Smart people simplify their writing. Take the upper-case cursive letter *q*. Whoever saw anything so silly looking as a $\mathcal{Q}$? It is much easier for the upper-case cursive *q* to be Q with its tail connecting to the following letter. Do not browbeat the child who simplifies legibly. He should be congratulated or at least left alone. Simplification should be allowed wherever the child wishes as long as the letter is legible. Simplifications generally move cursives in the direction of printed letters by removing frills. A simplified initial cursive *d* would be d instead of $\mathcal{d}$, and a simplified final *y* would be y instead of y.

When all else fails there is still a trump card to play in eliminating writing problems. Eliminate writing! Use typing instead. We have discussed this above in reversals, and it should suffice to say that individual letters cannot be reversed or disoriented when typed, though of course they can be typed in the wrong order—the very bread and butter of proofreaders. The idea of tiny hands on typewriters tends to boggle the mind but the subject can and should be taught when writing is illegible (or nearly so) and nothing else seems to help. Typing is a valuable skill and the child should learn by standard typing procedures (Lloyd and Krevolin, 1966; Petit-clerc, 1973), not hunt and peck. Typing will not help spelling problems, but it certainly can help eliminate writing problems.

Spelling.

Spelling is the production of words whose letter names or shapes are in correct order as determined by a dictionary. In the introduction to this chapter, we discussed the various levels and connections between writing and spelling and suggested that these were related to the sequence of remedial steps in reading. To spell correctly, one must be able to match by shape, letter-name with mental images and mental sounds, perhaps have some skill at phonics, and—if the spelling word is to be written—have developed the appropriate muscle-learning. Thus, many of the remedies that are useful for the learning-disabled pupil in reversals, in the various levels of reading problems, and in writing, are useful for spelling disabilities also.

If spelling is no better than reading, your priority will be reading. In many cases, spelling will improve as reading does without any special attention being given to it. Don't count on it, however. Some learning-disabled pupils who eventually take off in reading are immobilized on the launching pad in spelling. The same is true of writing. A pupil who is learning-disabled in writing may learn to execute the letter shapes legibly enough, though he may continue to misspell. Learning disability in spelling can have an effect on writing. Some learning-disabled pupils recognize they cannot spell a word, and their writing immediately changes from legible to what you might expect the web of an LSD-taking spider to be. We are not talking about the age-old pupil trick of making letters ambiguous on written spelling tests, hoping to get the benefit of the doubt if fatigue has sufficiently dulled your senses. When some learning-disabled pupils recognize they cannot spell a word, their written products may become unrecognizable as letters. Others maintain their poise and resort to legible attempts at phonetic spelling which are sure to be highly unusual at times, not to say bizarre, when compared with dictionary spellings. Compared to genuine phonetic spellings, though, they often make good sense. Anyone knows "cat" should be spelled "kat" and "light" should be spelled "lite," and they would be if something like the Initial Teaching Alphabet (Downing, 1964; O'Halloran, 1973) were in use. Again we advocate the introduction of ITA, but we must tear ourselves away from this hope and return to the subject of spelling in all-too-nonphonetic English.

If the learning disability in spelling is mild, simple color-cues and some tracing-saying may work. You circle the incorrect letter in color, draw the pupil's attention to it, and use a bit of tracing-saying. For more difficult cases exactly the same procedure is followed, but in an intensified form. You may print the difficult word with the "hard part" in a distinctive color. This printing is done large on a lined card of coarse paper. The pupil repeatedly traces the word with his forefinger while saying the letters. Eventually, if the word has more than one syllable or is phonetic, the parts of the word rather than the letters can be said while the tracing proceeds as before. Finally the pupil reaches the level of saying the whole word while doing the tracing. You should repeat the whole procedure then with the pupil tracing with his pencil rather than his finger. You might even use the pencil for the entire procedure; some experimentation will be necessary to see what produces the speediest and most long-lasting learning. Then it is time to have the pupil write the word *from memory*. If he does so correctly, lavish praise on him, add the word to his word bank, and shortly thereafter in the same session review the word with pencil tracing–saying. Then have the pupil write it several more times from memory until it appears automatic. Schedule further reviews later, and do not wait long. This helps deal with the maddening knew-it-yesterday-can't-spell-it-today affliction.

Various other techniques help in remedying spelling disabilities. Simply taping an alphabet to the pupil's desk for him to scan may help him hit upon a correct letter in those instances in which he realizes he needs one. Truly phonetic words can be presented in color-cues, with the initial sound in green, the final in red, medial short vowels in yellow, medial long vowels in brown. Medial consonants and blends probably are best left uncolored since you do not want to get a color system so difficult that it inspires a whole new learning disability of its own. Nonphonetic words are best done with the "trick parts" in color(s).

Filling in the blanks and flash presentation are good techniques for forcing attention to detail and giving practice in making the correct response in the correct sequence. With the word "cat," for instance, the tracing–saying has taken place and now it is time for a review. Write " __ at" and require the child to write in and say the correct letter. Make a whole string of these fill-ins, such as "c __ t," "ca __," "c __ __," " __ a __ ," " __ __ t," and " __ __ __ ." You can also use flash presentations in which you first show a card for a few seconds with a word already learned printed on it. The pupil looks, and after you take the card away, he writes the word from memory. The time span between taking away the card and the writing can be increased, which is easier than trying to speed up the flash presentation itself. That is hard to do without an actual tachistoscope. If your school or your district's division of instruction has one, you might use it. After flash presentation of the whole word, you present the same word the same way, but one letter is left blank. The pupil has to write down the missing letter. Another kind of fill-in is having the child read a note with all the vowels omitted. You can make it a classroom game maybe, with the children passing such notes and filling in the missing vowels to read the messages. Be careful to let the children know that this is the only note-passing time you allow and that it is really just a fun way of learning spelling. Otherwise you are sure eventually to hear some vaguely hostile murmurings about "What kind of school are you running over there," with the children being encouraged to pass notes.

We recommend teaching the learning-disabled child to use the dictionary. His age and intelligence will be factors in his success in this endeavor, but even early primary grade pupils can learn to use simple dictionaries, especially ones with lots of pictures. If an alphabet chart is on the wall or taped to his desk or inside his study carrel, he will at least have some idea about the sequence in the dictionary even if he's a bit shaky on saying the alphabet orally. The best alphabet chart might have the tricky lower-case letters (*b, d, p, q, n, u, m, w*) all in different colors so they can more readily be spotted as distinctive.

The child should have the use of his own dictionary at his desk. If he cannot guess the first few letters of a word he wants to write, encourage him to ask you, then to go to the dictionary. If you make it hard for him, he will choose a simpler word, which will not be desirable in terms of vocabulary building or in learning to express himself. Regrettably, the dictionary does not work for those who do not know what they do not know, but it is handy to have around. A picture dictionary is good since the child will casually browse through it, spy some intriguing picture, and perhaps learn a new word.

A plurals chart may help both the learning-disabled and the regular pupil in spelling. It could be posted on the wall or a smaller version taped to the pupil's desk or inside the study carrel.

How to Make Plurals

1. Regular words add "s."
2. Words ending in *s, ch, sh,* and *x* add "es."
3. Words ending in *vowel (a, e, i, o, u + y)* add "s."
4. Words ending in *consonant + y* usually end, when plural, in "ies."
5. Words ending in *f* or *fe* usually end, when plural, in "ves."
6. Some words change form: *Mouse* changes to "mice," and *man* to "men."
7. Some words do not change when plural: Sheep, deer, fish.

13. Arithmetic

MOST LEARNING-DISABLED children are significantly better in arithmetic than in reading, writing, and spelling. This is not strange when you consider it. There are only ten number shapes to learn, and, individually, their names always make the same sounds except 0, which is called "zero" or pronounced like the letter it resembles. You can count to a million with only thirty separate number names. The rules of counting are simple and counting is not usually a big deal. Matching by shape and naming are vastly easier in arithmetic than in the language areas. The whole business about mental images and mental sounds is much simpler in arithmetic because there are fewer numbers to worry about. Blissfully, there is no such thing as traditional phonics in arithmetic. No one ever sounded out "21" since numbers only have names, not sounds. "21" is always named twenty-one. These seem to us the reasons arithmetic is easier than reading for most learning-disabled pupils—until word problems come along.

Arithmetic is not without its troubles, however. Generally the troubles are not at the very simple levels of matching and naming, but at the levels of rote memory and of understanding the processes. Where matching by shape and number-naming are difficulties, follow exactly the same procedures you follow in remedying problems with their counterparts in alphabet letters. Where the child reverses numbers, use color-cues and tracing–saying exactly as you would in reading, writing, and spelling.

In adding number-names to the muscle-learning needed to make the numbers, you doubtless will have seen various more or less unpoetic rhyme systems telling how to make the numbers. They may be more trouble than they are worth for most learning-disabled children, who will profit from regular tracing–saying. Then again, some of them may be edified as well as charmed by the rhymes. These rhymes will not be a wall chart since any child who could read aloud well enough to read the chart would certainly be capable of making the numbers. It must be orally administered in combination with chalkboard demonstration and skywriting; we hope our own dubious version will not be too hard for you to swallow. Improve upon it if you can.

Making Numbers

1. A tall straight stick makes a 1.
   A straight line 1 is fun.
2. Around and back
   On a railroad track.
   2! 2! 2!

3. Around a tree
   And around a tree
   Makes a 3.
4. Go down halfway and then go right.
   Then make a 1 and the 4 is in sight.
5. Number 5 has a little round tummy.
   He wears a cap that looks so funny.
6. Down to a loop,
   And a 6 rolls a hoop.
7. Across the sky and down from heaven.
   That makes the number 7.
8. Make a big S, but do not wait.
   Go back to the start and you've got an 8.
9. A loop and a line
   Makes 9.
10. One number looks like a hole.
    It's the 0 (read "zero").

Remediation of arithmetic learning disabilities is easier than that of language learning disabilities for another reason not mentioned above. Arithmetic can very easily be made concrete. That reason is itself the primary principle in approaching an arithmetic learning disability: *make the remedial process as concrete as you can once you have specified the target.* Begin all new arithmetic activities with concrete manipulative materials, such as an abacus. We will illustrate this principle below as we trace arithmetic from its most basic concepts to higher grammar school levels. At any one of these levels learning disability may make itself known. To remedy a higher-level disability effectively, you may not have to go all the way back to the start although many times you must. This principle of concreteness is impossible to follow very well, if at all, if you are trying to teach the new math, since the new math is rather abstract and has little perceivable relation to the real world. The arithmetic learning-disabled child will be hopelessly lost in the new math. He may never understand set theory, much less be able to add and subtract, but then, many of the regular pupils learning the new math never learn to do that very well either (Jastak and Jastak, 1965; Kline, 1974). Having a pupil learning-disabled in arithmetic in your class may even be a boon to you. It could give you the reason you've been waiting for to contribute your new math material to the next Boy or Girl Scout paper drive and get back to teaching kids to add and subtract.

To do any arithmetic the child must have the concepts of "more" and "less," and almost all children have those concepts when they get to school. A few, including some very learning-disabled ones, will not. Use buttons, washers, blocks, jacks, or abacus beads to teach these two ideas. Cuisenaire rods are excellent for this (Cuisenaire Company of America, Inc., 12 Church St., New Rochelle, NY 10805). The idea of quantity should not be too difficult to teach concretely except to extremely disabled children. Next, the pupil should learn matching, and then the number names by tracing-saying if need be. By tracing-saying most pupils will learn the muscle-movements, but the number-making rhymes can be trotted out if required. Skywriting may also be employed, with or without the rhymes.

Next, the pupil should learn rote recital of the number names (counting) from one to as high as he wants to go. Little children love to count high. A parent, however, may come to have mixed emotions after the seventh or eighth time the child counts to one thousand. Counting does have to be accomplished by rote, as in the case of the alphabet—though the alphabet at least has a singing rhyme—and it is best done by having the child mimic you. You might first say, "One"; the child says, "One." You say, "Two"; the child says, "Two," and so on. Then you move to groups, brief at first, as "One, two, three," with the child repeating after you. Gradually you build up the rote ability. Always point to the numbers as you count, which helps solidify number-naming. Then begin to point randomly to numbers to check the child's real knowledge of the names. Some children can count by rote without being able to identify all the numbers by sight. Use tracing-saying and more rote learning if the child's knowledge is shaky at this stage. You are teaching, not testing, so give as much help as needed until the child can do it himself.

Next comes the matter of attaching quantities to the written symbols. Forcing puzzles are useful here:

and so forth. The abacus, holding up fingers, and making dots on the page help too. Use as many concrete ways as you can think of to associate quantities with their written symbols.

SIMPLE ADDITION AND SUBTRACTION

Once more and less, matching, number names, rote counting, and symbols for quantities are learned, it is time to move into addition. Teach the plus sign first and the horizontal layout for addition problems. Teach the child how to read the problem before you teach him to do it. Have him read aloud after you again and again a string of simple addition problems such as $2 + 2$, $3 + 2$, $4 + 5$, and so on. Tell him these are addition problems and have him learn the name. Color-cue the plus sign. Show the child what the plus means by concrete processes. Show him two abacus beads, then say, "Plus two," while moving two more beads over to the first two. Have the child count the total number of beads. Let us assume his answer is "four." If it is, congratulate him by saying, "Good, you have added two plus two and the answer is four." Have him do the whole thing by himself. Show him how to do the same thing on his fingers or by putting dots on the page. You might illustrate $2 + 2 = 4$ like this .. + .. = ... Illustrate with a number line:

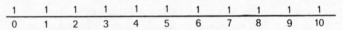

Have the child count to two, pointing as he counts. Then say, "Count two *more*." When he has done so, ask, "What number are you on now?" It should, of course, be four. An accordionfold can be helpful also:

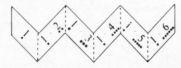

and so forth. It is probably best to keep the rows of dots horizontal at first since dots are easier to count that way and it builds left-to-right eye movements in the child.

Use these crutches repeatedly until simple horizontal addition is thoroughly learned. It will be becoming more automatic and you can speed up the process with flash cards. Use regular flash cards, but allow, even encourage, the child to count on his fingers or use any other crutch to get the correct answer. Eventually it will be automatic. Then you can teach full horizontal addition where the only new element is the equals sign. You can use a dot system like this: $\ddot{2} + \ddot{2} =$ 4, and after putting four dots over the 4 ($\ddot{4}$), ask, "Is the equals sign happy?" In mathematics it is vital for the equals sign to be happy. After that you can go to the vertical layout of addition covered in the following section.

Subtraction comes next and will be easier to teach if the child is really firm in the concepts of more and less. "Take away" should be the first name for the minus sign. Illustrate concretely and do all the things you did for horizontal addition problems. When the child can do it, teach the vertical version. About now you can break the news that " – " is also called minus. Have the child read problems saying minus instead of take away until he knows they are the same.

Bringing Down, Carrying, and Borrowing

The child eventually must come to addition problems where one of the numbers to be added has two digits, but do not begin with problems which require "carrying." Your first aim is to teach the pupil that in arithmetic one begins on the right. Color-cuing is used to do this. Make a green vertical mark to the right of the problems. Remind the pupil that green always means "go" or "start here." Teach the pupil then how to bring down the leftmost digit in the upper sum to be added. Use graph paper in which the numbers are in separate squares. This way you can teach the child that only one number in the answer can go into the square beneath each column; eventually this principle will be expanded to other columns to the left in more difficult problems.

After bringing down is firmly learned, move boldly to carrying problems. Use the graph paper method again with only one number allowed in each answer square. We advocate the old-fashioned method of simply writing the carried number over the next column to the left. Show the child how to add it with the other number in that column. Once the answer is obtained, use concrete methods such as an abacus to show the child that it is the correct answer. Allow the use of any crutches. If the child insists upon making seventeen dots, then nine dots in $\begin{array}{r} 17 \\ +9 \end{array}$, that is all right if his total count reaches twenty-six. You might suggest it would be quicker to start with seventeen in his head, then to make nine dots on paper and count them, with the first of the nine counted "eighteen," and so on to twenty-six. A faster version would be to count as the nine dots are made. Tapping is all right too if the child has a good enough feel for it. Tell him to start with seventeen in his head, then tap nine times, counting up from seventeen at each of the nine taps. The taps will have to be grouped into, say, three groups of three. This is a highly advanced crutch and not too many children will be able to use it. Those who can will be on the verge of doing the whole thing mentally.

Subtraction problems such as $\begin{array}{r} 74 \\ -3 \end{array}$, with two-digit minuends and one-digit subtrahends which do not require borrowing, come next. These will not be too difficult since all they amount to is subtracting a one-digit subtrahend from the second digit of the minuend, and bringing down the first digit of the minuend. Illustrate it all concretely just to make sure the pupil understands, and you should use the graph paper method as well as the abacus.

The big hurdle is next, where borrowing is required. It is best to use graph paper again, and begin with problems with two-digit minuends and one-digit subtrahends. Illustrate with abacus beads that the one-digit subtrahend cannot be taken away from the rightmost digit of the minuend since there are not enough beads. Then illustrate with abacus beads that the subtrahend *can* be taken away from the whole minuend. Allow a few moments for the pupil to absorb the full impact of this baffling piece of information. Tell him that it can be done without the beads. Sadly, it is not too easy, but do not tell him that. We advocate visual regrouping. This brings in the business about "tens" and "ones," but there is no way to put it off forever. An abacus is invaluable here, but you can do it like this. Take $\begin{smallmatrix}26\\-9\end{smallmatrix}$. Make an illustration of this sort:

STEP ONE

TENS	ONES	
$\|\|$	$\|\|\|\|\|\|$	$= 26$
	$\|\|\|\|\|\|\|\|\|$	$= \dfrac{9}{?}$

STEP TWO

TENS	ONES	
$\cancel{\|}\|$	$\|\|\|\|\|\|\|\|\|\|\|\|\|\|\|\|$	$= 26$
	$\|\|\|\|\|\|\|\|$	$= \dfrac{9}{?}$

STEP THREE

TENS	ONES	
$\|$	$\cancel{\|}\cancel{\|}\cancel{\|}\cancel{\|}\cancel{\|}\cancel{\|}\cancel{\|}\cancel{\|}\cancel{\|}\|\|\|\|\|\|$	$= 17$
	$\cancel{\|}\cancel{\|}\cancel{\|}\cancel{\|}\cancel{\|}\cancel{\|}\cancel{\|}\cancel{\|}\cancel{\|}$	

       1   7

Show how one mark in the tens column becomes ten marks when moved over to the ones column. Do it. Make ten new marks in the ones column and erase or mark out one of them in the tens column. That done, show the pupil how to cross out as many marks in the new minuend of the ones column as there are in the unchanged subtrahend ones column. He now counts the number of marks left in the new ones minuend column and enters that remaining number in the ones column answer box. Then show him how to bring down the number of marks left in the changed tens column of the minuend. After a number of illustrations, the pupil should be able to do it himself. Always accompany these illustrations with the actual problem in numbers. It is so much easier to do all this with an abacus that we cannot recommend too often that you obtain one. The regular children will profit from it as much as the learning-disabled. You might order a catalog, such as that offered by Developmental Learning Materials (7440 Natchez Ave., Niles, IL 60648), and look over a large abacus. It is to be hoped that the concept of borrowing will be taught in this way. Just because the concept is taught and the operation performed with abacus beads or the tens–ones visual-regrouping system, it does not mean the child always can do it with numbers alone at this stage.

It is now time to try to transfer all this business from the abacus and visual-regrouping systems to the use of numbers alone. You may not accomplish this for quite a long while, but as always, encourage the use of all crutches as long as the pupil needs them. Keep the abacus at hand. Return to the graph paper. Simple problems where the answer is two digits, as in

$\begin{array}{r} 26 \\ -9 \end{array}$, are not much more difficult than problems where the

answer is one digit, as in $\begin{array}{r} 17 \\ -9 \end{array}$, if you use the graph paper approach that works so well in addition. That is because there is nothing for the child to do but count from nine to seventeen and enter that number of counts, eight, as the answer. He may have to make seventeen marks, then cross off nine of them, then count the remaining marks. You might also use a number line to show the pupil that subtraction is counting backward (to the left on the number line) from the larger number (minuend) to the smaller number (subtrahend) and the answer is the number of counts needed to reach the subtrahend. With $\begin{array}{r} 26 \\ -9 \end{array}$, show how to change the two to a one through borrowing, and enter the borrowed one above the two's box, with the two having been crossed out. The borrowed ten units (numeral 1) are then placed to the left of the 6 in the one's box. The child then counts, by a mark system or other crutch, from nine to sixteen and enters that number of counts under the nine. Then he brings down the one, which had been a two. A graphic portrayal is in order.

STEP ONE	TENS	ONES
	2	6
	-	9

STEP TWO	TENS	ONES
	1	
	2̸	16
	-	9

STEP THREE	TENS	ONES
	↗1	
brought down		16
	-	9
	1	7

This is a tedious affair at best. With prolonged use of crutches, borrowing in subtraction may become more automatic for the learning-disabled pupil. Flash card practice combined with tracing–saying can be used and will assist in making answers automatic in simpler problems. If nothing works after prolonged effort, we see no harm in the pupil's using crutches on a permanent basis. Math will never be his long suit anyway, so little would be gained by interpreting the affair as a catastrophe. Then again, some of the pupils who are learning-disabled in arithmetic take off eventually just as sometimes happens in reading. One of us had a minor learning disability in not being able to add or subtract mentally anything involving a nine well into junior high, and was using an effective and very carefully camouflaged tapping system. When algebra was reached, however, general performance in math blossomed and the addition and subtraction difficulty with nine unaccountably disappeared. So let the pupil severely disabled in arithmetic use his crutches if he must. If ever he can cast them off, fine; if not, you will have prevented undue scarring in a child who might be successful in more important things, such as reading.

MULTIPLICATION

Having expressed that high-sounding sentiment, let us return to the grind and what comes next, multiplication. The trick in multiplication is to recognize that it is counting forward in groups, just as division is counting backward in groups. If pupils learning-disabled in arithmetic have become quite firm in addition, multiplication will not be a real trial until complex problems are reached which have boundless opportunities for computational errors in addition. But that could happen to anyone.

With multiplication, first have the pupil read aloud dozens of problems such as 3 x 2 and $\begin{array}{r}3\\\times2\end{array}$ until he knows the times sign. Move right into the vertical layout. The kid will already know that the horizontal layout doesn't get him far in addition and subtraction. Then tell him that multiplication is a short way of adding and that anyone who can add can multiply. Do not tell him that this may only be after many hours of practice! Set up the problem as an addition problem. Illustrate it on the abacus. Move right into flash cards, but adjacent to $\times 2$ $\overset{3}{}$ have $+3$ $\overset{3}{}$ also. The pupil can add $+3$ $\overset{3}{}$ and thus knows the answer, but have him read $\times 2$ $\overset{3}{}$ and give the answer, six. Teach the smaller numbers in the times tables that way and begin to phase out the $+3$ $\overset{3}{}$ part. Eventually the smaller numbers become rote. Tell the child you will teach him the rest of the times tables by tracing–saying and flash cards. Print, for instance, $\frac{\times 6}{30}$ $\overset{5}{}$ (read as "five times six equals thirty") on a large card of fairly rough paper and follow the usual tracing–saying routine. Review often and require performance from memory. Finally use regular flash cards with the vertical presentation and with the answer on the back of the card, which you will flip over to give the child immediate feedback on his answer. Teach the entire times table this way. It takes a while, and perhaps someone else can help you. Always make sure each step is firmly taken before going on to the next. When real problems are reached, use graph paper and the usual carrying procedure of entering the number to be carried over the next column to the left in the multiplicand. Keep only one number in each square of the graph paper. The rest is addition.

DIVISION

Division is counting backward in groups; you cannot divide if you cannot multiply and subtract. Those latter two operations must be firmly established before division can be learned successfully. Few, if any children will have a learning disability that comes to light for the first time in division. They will have been discovered before in arithmetic's foundations in matching and so on, in addition, subtraction, or multiplication. You cannot move them into division without a thorough grounding in these other, more important skills. Quite possibly the whole business of arithmetic will have become, if not quite automatic, at least rather so, by the time division is reached.

If there is a division difficulty, use graph paper once again. Naturally begin with short division. Teach the child that to divide is to guess what number as the quotient will be equal to or less than the dividend when multiplied by the divisor. Leave it at that. Illustrate it repeatedly. Let him experiment; he will get the idea. You can go the tracing–saying and flash card route then for simple division problems to make them automatic, pointing out that division is multiplication backwards. The same procedure, but incorporating the subtraction process, will go into long division, and we recommend the same general process. Use graph paper, but obviously tracing–saying and flash cards are out. Trial and error will have to prevail until the operation becomes more automatic.

14. Dos and Don'ts for Teachers and Parents

WE HAVE SAID all we are going to about academics. We have tried to be as specific as we could about academics after providing the basic assumptions and principles for a practical approach to learning disabilities remedies. Much in this chapter has already been said or implied, but review is the mainstay of memory. Besides that, there is something new here: tips you can give parents, particularly on matters of homework and behavior management. So bear with us here as we regroup some of our ideas to present a cracker-barrel style list of dos and don'ts. Some items apply more to school, some more to home, and some about equally to both fronts. We will use a code of *T* and *P* for teacher and parent respectively to expedite your reference to the list as you prepare for parent conferences. Further help may be found in a little booklet for teachers and parents (Weiss and Weiss, 1973).

(T,P)

1) Don't compare the learning-disabled child to other children within the classroom or the home. To do so all but automatically leads to defeat and defeatism on the part of the learning-disabled child. Each one has a right to be himself with his own pattern of abilities. When you encourage competition, have the child compete with his own past performance. Goals and expectations also should be set for the child in terms of his past performance.

(T,P)

2) Don't regard the child with disfavor when he uses crutches such as pointing at words with his finger, using a straightedge in reading, using dots in arithmetic, or using lined paper to write letters. Construct crutches and encourage the child in their use. This is the basis of successful remedies. The child will give up the crutches when he is able to do so.

(T,P)

3) Don't put pressure on the child to learn quickly, since pressure disorganizes rather than helps him. Don't pressure the child to read rapidly. Allow him to read at his own speed. Speed may be increased only on material which is very easy for the child. Do see that the child has material on which he obtains 80 to 90 percent comprehension. Read to the child at home and let him see you reading in the course of your everyday life. Try novel approaches to helping your child with reading (Slosson, 1963; Weiss and Weiss, 1973).

(T)

4) Don't give in to the child's urging for you to go faster or to give more new work than in your judgment he can handle. Don't overload the learning system. Do praise him

for his progress and enthusiasm, but suggest another activity at his capability level.

(T,P)

5) Don't become angry or impatient with the child. When you do so, the cause generally will be unrealistic expectations on your part. It will scare the child and connect the learning process with unpleasantness. Reassure him and praise something he has done correctly or made a good effort to do. The child with learning disabilities is more dependent on your approval than are most children the same age.

(T,P)

6) Don't make the child feel inadequate when he forgets work you thought he had learned. This will happen frequently, so resist that urge to grit your teeth and rattle his. Review often and point out every little bit of progress you can. Keep an optimistic air. Remember that what is learned by rote memory may not be retained for long without frequent review.

(T,P)

7) Don't feel personally slighted if the child gets upset or becomes stubborn or otherwise displays temper. If you lose control too, it will only make the situation worse, and you will provide the worst kind of model of what to do when frustrated. Do change activities when you see signs of definite frustration coming on. Remember that short, frequent practice sessions are always better than long sessions once or twice a week.

(T,P)

8) While schedules should always be set up and followed exactly whenever possible, don't try to make the child study

when he is tired or overexcited. Do wait until he is calm and rested. Make maximum use of his premium time on good days when he is accessible and relaxed. On relatively bad days you may be able to review some material that has been mastered already.

(T)

9) Don't emphasize spelling and writing at the expense of reading. Don't emphasize penmanship. Remember that your chief goal is to improve the child's ability to comprehend the written word.

(T)

10) Give praise for jobs well done and for effort, even if unsuccessful. Unearned praise is a waste. Don't step aside until the child appears to be able to work on his own, but then do so while watching from a distance. Do study behavior modification books for techniques you can use in the classroom. Consult your school psychologist about them.

(T,P)

11) Be consistent with discipline, demands, routines, and promises. If you must punish, do it right away and make it appropriate to the infraction. Don't punish in anger. Don't punish with homework. Do explain that the punishment is to help him learn not to get into trouble again. Use time-out or positive practice wherever you can. Ask your school psychologist about other alternatives to traditional punishment. Remember, the learning-disabled child is not learning-disabled because he is bad, but because your teaching techniques aren't working with him. Blaming the child will have no effect other than to create guilt, worry, and hard feelings.

(T,P)

12) When the child makes a request, decide immediately whether or not to grant it. Don't give in to nagging. Don't get drawn into arguments about the logic or fairness of your decisions. Do strive for logic and fairness in your decisions! When in doubt, talk the situation over with other teachers, parents, or with your school psychologist. Teach the meaning of *no* by not giving in after you say it.

(T,P)

13) Avoid situations in which you have to be saying *no* often. Plan ahead to avoid such situations, and distract the child from undesirable behavior by offering suggestions about other things he could be doing.

(P)

14) Don't criticize the school's program or the teacher in front of the child. If you do so, don't be surprised if the child develops a don't-care attitude, or worse. Do offer to give the teacher assistance. Do keep in contact with the teacher. Don't say things like, "I always hated school (arithmetic) (my teachers) too."

(T)

15) Do give the parents specifics when they ask how to help. Do break down what you give them into small steps, and do see that they know exactly how to take each step. Do keep in close contact if they help on homework; give them only a small assignment at one time. Don't say things like, "Oh, you can help him in spelling," and leave it at that. Don't say, "There's really no way you can help." The parents are valuable allies in doing your job, and they are just as interested

in the child's progress as you are. Give them material to use at home. Tell them where to order phonics kits, linguistic readers, an abacus, or whatever, and how to use a study carrel at home.

(P)

16) Don't pump your child about what went on at school. If he wants to talk about it, he will. If he doesn't want to talk about it and you force the issue, it will just cause an unpleasant scene and make the child even less likely to talk about school spontaneously. If you want to know more, contact the teacher.

(P)

17) It is better for parents to help their children by reviewing material the child has already covered. Don't try to do it in a way different from the teacher's. If you undermine the teacher, don't be puzzled when the child ignores the teacher's instructions. Do try to find out from the teacher how you can help. Do follow his or her suggestions.

(P)

18) Don't take the child's homework out of his hands without being certain he wants your help. Don't do so unless you know how to help. The child needs to feel your confidence that he can learn. Learning-disabled children learn through special procedures, and their learning speed is slower than that of the regular child, so don't push too hard. Do offer help in a friendly, courteous way. Do have a fixed time and place for homework. Have the place quiet. Require work before play. Find out from the teacher or your school psychologist how to use incentive systems (Patterson and Gullion, 1968).

(P,T)

19)   If you can tell that the child's homework is too difficult for him, contact the teacher. He or she would be happy if you read most of the lesson to the child and then discussed it with him rather than letting him agonize over it for hours and still not know what it meant. It will then be up to the teacher to revise the amount and type of homework.

(T)

20)   Do allow and encourage the child to seek help from other children (not on tests, of course!). Children sometimes have the most ingeniously simple shortcuts and crutches for learning. Find a good child tutor for the learning-disabled.

15. Resources

You MAY NOT need us to tell you, but you are going to need help with many cases of learning disability you encounter in your classroom. Optimally yours is a school system with a strong special education program for learning-disabled pupils, with resource rooms and mobile resource teachers, and with a full complement of school psychologists, teachers' aides, speech therapists, remedial reading teachers, school nurses, and so forth. But what about the other 99 percent of schools, you ask? You must turn elsewhere, even in systems which have some but not enough of these resources, if you are to make headway.

The chief point to keep in mind is that willingness to help and ability to teach do not automatically mean a person can effectively remedy learning disabilities. After all, the child already has had teachers who were ready, willing, and able to try, but there he sits in your classroom, just as he did in theirs. You must guide your helper so that his or her willingness and ability can be used effectively. To do this, you must develop lesson plans for the helper just as you must develop them for yourself.

Let us assume that you and your school psychologist have worked out a plan of attack by specifying the goal, breaking the distance between pupil as-is and the goal into steps, choosing your materials and all the rest of it. When you or your school psychologist enlist your helper you must tell him or her what to do, how to do it, how to know it has been done, and what to do then. You are structuring the whole affair for the helper just as you structure it for the pupil. You are teaching the helper how to help.

Do not under any condition set the program up for the helper and then let the helper go his or her own way. Arrange frequent feedback sessions. You must arrange for observation of the actual tutoring too. Observation may have to be carried out every other session at first. It's time consuming, but it more than pays for itself in the long run. Frequent sessions are necessary to keep the helper on the track, to show your appreciation, and to set up future steps or replan those which have not worked.

People offer their services because they want to. Some will do so for the money alone; that is fine if they get results and if the school system, the PTA, or the child's parents have the money. Quite frankly, to get and keep someone good over a period of time usually takes money. Most helpers will have a combination of reasons: community spirit, liking for children, a desire to ease needless suffering, the wish for approval for an important and difficult job well done, a need to express creativity, simple curiosity and liking for challenge, money, and other reasons. They may have all this, but they do not have instinctive knowledge in the remediation of learning disabilities. You must help them or they will come to feel lost and to be lost. If you do not keep in close contact, they may become discouraged or feel ignored and unappreciated. Stick with them or don't be surprised at dropouts, no results, or even in a few instances, negative results.

If you let the helper go and get negative results, the decline and fall will tend to go like this: left to his or her own devices and having met some obstacles, the helper may revert to home-brews, hodgepodge tutoring, and implausible explanations of the learning disability to guide efforts which end as quite misguided. For instance, after two months of tutoring for a severe problem in reversals, and with no contact from you or the school psychologist, you may hear the helper voice the opinion that it is "a home problem," that the parents have not given the child the attention he needed. You may hear this from the stunned parents who the helper thought would be helped by the information. The parents may be angry or let down; you may be disappointed with the helper (who had looked so promising); and the helper may be indignant or hurt and may bid you farewell. Worst of all, the child will not have learned much. What caused all this? Lack of feedback on the part of you and your school psychologist. You and the school psychologist must specifically plan the helping of the helper.

We have made the point amply that your helper needs frequent feedback and guidance, but you must first find the helper. Here are some suggestions of places to look and people to ask:

1) Your district may have lists of "approved" tutors, but remember that being a tutor or being a teacher does not imply

there are automatic skills in learning disabilities remediation.

2) Contact your local volunteer bureau or your local retired teachers association.

3) Broadcast an appeal at a PTA meeting.

4) If there is a nearby university, call the education, special education, educational psychology, and psychology departments and ask for a learning-disabilities tutor.

5) If you live near a military base, you have a potential gold mine. Servicemen and women (and their spouses) who may not really feel part of your community will be eager and gratified to contribute. Call the continuing education office, call the human relations office, call the officers' and NCOs' and enlisted men's wives' clubs, call the chaplains. Call the Commanding Officer if you must. Get the word out and a response is almost guaranteed. (Military bases are also good hunting for "big brother–big sister" candidates.)

6) For a change of pace, go to a meeting of your board of education. In these days someone may very well be standing up and berating the board for its lack of provision of special education for the learning-disabled. Take that person's name. Catch him or her after the meeting or call the next day.

7) A college student or bright high school student might do. Put in calls to high school and college counselors and ask them whether they know of any likely prospects.

8) Use grammar school children. An older child in your school or an exceptional one in your own room may be able to do much more than you ever thought possible.

9) Use the LD child's parents. It is best not to use the child's own parents if patterns of mutual irritation over school work have built up. If such patterns have built up and if you have two learning-disabled children, exchange the parents. You and

another teacher can exchange parents if you each have one learning-disabled child.

10) Contact civic organizations, service clubs, and religious groups.

11) Advertise. A newspaper ad may bring in just the right person.

16. Summary

This guide was written for use with school children who have a certain type of problem. Learning disability seems to us the best name for it, since it refers to what is observed by you and the school psychologists as the problem. We expect something like teaching/learning disability will be its new name before long. Problems are seen and heard, not assumed, so we dispensed with the many fancy theories and approaches to remediation that assume the real problem underlies and is different from the observed one. Today teachers and parents demand results in the classroom and the study carrel, not theories from the armchair. Ivory tower theories and esoteric practices have all the marks of a dead duck.

Remedies must be addressed to the observed problems. Since most remediation is done by regular teachers—you—the remedial techniques must be stated in terms understandable to those who have to use them, namely yourselves. Since the problem is defined by your observations, your observations must be descriptively specific. In working with the school psychologist, you should list priorities if more than one general type of problem is observed. Practically every problem is distinctive to some degree, so the remedies are always individualized. You must maintain a flexible, experimental frame of mind in devising remedies. Regular materials and methods have not worked with the learning-disabled child, so you must teach him in a different, individualized way.

Aside from the fact that they are hard to teach, the only characteristic common to all learning-disabled children is that their disabilities are specific. There are deficits, gaps, and oddities in the learning pattern which cannot be explained by lack of intellectual ability, emotional problems, the parents, the previous teachers, you, or underachievement. Other troublesome characteristics may or may not be present with learning disability. Many learning-disabled children show conceptual and perceptual deficits, hyperactivity in its various forms, poor memory, visual inefficiency, poor body image, and certain emotional problems. We described these and other characteristics and addressed the question of whether remedying these problems helps to remedy the specific learning disabilities themselves.

Weak links occur in the chain between identifying the learning-disabled child and helping him. Psychologists' psychologese, school systems' lack of special classes, and teachers' handwashing were mentioned. This guide attempted to remedy the problem of jargon. Money and pressure, neither of them sure things, may remedy the school systems' lack of resources. You teachers must now abandon the excuse about "thirty others" and realize how much you can learn from your most difficult pupils.

After you identify the learning-disabled pupil, you probably will initiate a referral. You first consult cumulative records and previous teachers, then you hold a conference with your principal, and following that with the child's parents. Parental approval must be obtained before you have the green light to get a psychological assessment. You must fill out forms and fill in the child as to what is going to happen and why.

Your school psychologist enters the scene next. Interaction between you and your school psychologist should be in person, not on paper. The psychologist should see work samples from the child and may observe him in the classroom. He or she will then probably put the student through a battery of tests. The results should come to you speedily, and personal conferences about the results must take place to work out ways of putting words into action. Results must be presented to the child's parents and to the child.

The remediation process has three principal conditions. First, the goal of remediation must be specified if there is to be much chance of its being attained or of knowing how close you have come to attaining it. This is important in maintaining motivation and direction. Second, the gap between pupil as-is and the goal must be divided into manageable steps under the old, but sound assumption that you must only bite off what you can chew. Third, decisions must be made about how to take the steps to reach the goal. You and the school psychologist share in all of these steps.

To get to where you want to go, there must be motivation on your part and on the pupil's. Much of your motivation will stem from seeing positive results, and it is no different with the pupil. However, artificial reward systems (which really aren't any more artificial than those that keep us all going, only more blatant) may need to be used with the pupil. This means you will be using behavior modification techniques. Your school psychologist will help adjust these techniques to your classroom's structure and the pupil's needs. Discipline of the child and of yourself must be maintained, and by this is meant structure and timed rewards. You can use alternatives to traditional punishment, such as time-out and positive practice, in many touchy management situations. Your expectations about the pupil's performance must be explicitly stated if the child is expected to meet them and if you are to know when he has.

Successful remediation of learning disabilities demands that you structure the learning environment in certain ways. Your classroom, or at least the learning-disabled pupil's position in it, must be structured to reduce distractions and to focus the pupil's attention. Study carrels are almost imperative in doing that. Your instructions must be so fashioned as to be explicit, concise, and organized in logical sequence if the child is to respond correctly to them. The model for doing this is programmed instruction. Your teaching materials must be individualized and concrete. Almost certainly they will be different from the regular materials on which the child is already failing. Your school psychologist will contribute ideas about the choice of materials.

The first kind of learning disability we specifically prescribed remedies for was reversals, which cuts across all academic areas. Tracing–saying, forced-attention left-to-right progression techniques and other tactics were described and recommended.

In reading disabilities, a sequence of levels was presented where you may discover problems and apply remedies. This sequence was matching by shape, letter-naming, mental images and mental sounds, phonics, and auditory discrimination. A distilled version of the practical remedial approach for learning disabilities in reading was presented. It was emphasized that the pupil must learn each remediation step to the point of its being automatic before proceeding to the next step. Length of steps and type of material depend upon the pupil's performance, which should be correct eight or nine times out of ten if motivation is to be maintained. It is extremely important that you review frequently with the learning-disabled child what he has learned. This builds a foundation of confidence as well as of academics. A section on the traditional reading problems of omissions, substitutions, additions, reversals, and word-calling was presented, and practical remedies were suggested for your use.

Next we dealt with the written product in language—writing and spelling. These two areas very much follow reading in terms of levels and remedies for the disabilities observable at the different levels. Writing and written spelling have the extra ingredient of muscle-learning. The places of penmanship, cursive, and typing were discussed.

Arithmetic claims fewer learning-disability victims than do the language areas until word problems set in. This is because arithmetic is non-phonetic and much more concrete than language. To make processes concrete is your guiding principle in remedying learning disabilities in arithmetic. The levels in arithmetic where disabilities occur and can be remedied are the concepts of "more" and "less," matching by shape, number-naming, rote counting, muscle-learning, and attaching quantities to symbols. Beyond those come our old friends—addition, subtraction, multiplication, and division. The uses to which you may put graph paper, the abacus, visual regrouping, and flash cards were discussed.

Dos and don'ts were presented both for you and for the parents of the children you teach. These mostly reviewed points already made; however, some extra suggestions regarding homework and behavior management were added. You can use some of these suggestions almost without modification in parent conferences.

To do what you must in learning-disabilities remediation, you are going to need helpers from time to time. First you must find the helper: we suggested places to look. Second, and equally important, you must train and closely follow the helper's activities. As it was with you in the beginning, so it is now with the helper. He or she deserves to be told exactly what to do, how to do it, how to know he or she has done it, and what to do next.

Afterword

As WE SAID in the Preface, this guide will not answer all your questions or solve all your classroom problems immediately. Some day that may be done. Some day teaching for all children will be individualized and know-how will be so complete that each child's optimum performance will be obtained by plugging him in at the proper computer-assisted teaching terminal or something of the sort. Maybe this will lead to the new high adventure in education of obtaining each person's best learning, so that creativity and individual expression can flower. The teacher will then be a guru of sorts. We hope it will be that way in the world to come. It could be that way, or the guru stage may never be reached. Society may settle for having the best educated children and not press on for having the most creative, most individual, and best educated children. It all depends on which values predominate. If the educational utopian guru stage does come, it will lead to a social utopia of the freest people ever. Knowledge provides alternatives, and to have alternatives is to be free. Whatever happens, advances in technology cannot be stopped in a free society. Make the most of them, and you will have the best chance of making the most of your pupils and of yourself.

At present we fall woefully short of even having the best educated children possible, much less the most creative and least homogenized ones. We hope this guide will lead toward a better chance and a better education for those children who have fallen by the wayside since education became compulsory and our society became literate and technological. This guide can help, but your creative cunning or that of someone else must take up where the guide leaves off.

Imagine that the most learning-disabled child possible is in your charge. A little girl, born deaf and blind, and your job is to educate her. Not just deficits or gaps in knowledge of academics, speech, and listening, but no knowledge of academics, no speech, no listening. Where are tracing-saying and phonics without hearing? Where are color-cues and visual regrouping without sight? But it can and has been done. The miracle of Anne Sullivan's teaching and Helen Keller's learning is known to you all. Whenever you feel your inspiration beginning to sag, read again of Anne Sullivan and Helen Keller. Then go back to work at producing miracles in your own classroom.

References

Arena, J. I. (Ed.) *Building handwriting skills in dyslexic children.* San Rafael, Calif.: Academic Therapy Publications, 1970.

Black, F. W. Achievement test performance of high and low perceiving learning disabled children. *Journal of Learning Disabilities,* 1974, *7,* 60–64.

Boder, E. Developmental dyslexia: Prevailing diagnostic concepts and a new diagnostic approach. In H. R. Myklebust (Ed.), *Progress in learning disabilities* (Volume II). New York: Grune and Stratton, 1971.

Bruininks, H., Glaman, G. M., & Clark, C. R. Issues in determining prevalence of reading retardation. *The Reading Teacher,* 1973, *27,* 177–185.

Bryan, T. H. Learning disabilities: A new stereotype. *Journal of Learning Disabilities,* 1974, *7,* 46–51.

Bryant, N. D. Learning disabilities. *The Instructor,* 1972, *81,* 49–65.

Buckley, N. K. and Walker, H. M. *Modifying classroom behavior.* Champaign, Ill.: Research Press, 1970.

Cohen, S. A. *Teach them all to read.* New York: Random House, 1969.

Conners, C. K., Eisenberg, L., & Barcai, A. Effect of dextroamphetamine on children: Studies on subjects with learning disabilities and school behavior problems. *Archives of General Psychiatry,* 1967, *17,* 478–485.

Cowgill, M. L., Friedland, S., & Shapiro, R. Predicting learning disabilities from kindergarten reports. *Journal of Learning Disabilities,* 1973, *6,* 50–55.

Critchley, M. *The dyslexic child* (2nd ed.). London: William Heinemann Medical Books, 1970.

Cruickshank, W. M. Myths and realities in learning disabilities. *Journal of Learning Disabilities,* 1977, *10,* 57–64.

Cutts, K. K., & Jasper, H. H. Effect of benzedrine sulfate on behavior-problem children with abnormal electroencephalograms. *Archives of Neurology and Psychiatry,* 1949, *41,* 1138–1145.

Della–Piana, G. M. *Reading diagnosis and prescription.* New York: Holt, Rinehart and Winston, 1968.

Divoky, D. Education's latest victim: The "LD" kid. *Learning,* October, 1974, pp. 20–25.

Downing, J. A. *The initial teaching alphabet reading experiment.* Palo Alto, Calif.: Scott, Foresman, 1964.

Durrell, D. D., & Murphy, H. A. *Speech-to-print phonics: A phonics foundation for reading.* New York: Harcourt Brace Jovanovich, Inc., 1972.

Eisenberg, J. Behavioral manifestations of cerebral damage in childhood. In H. G. Birch (Ed.), *Brain damage in childhood.* Baltimore: Williams and Wilkins, 1964.

Eisenson, J. *Examining for aphasia: A manual for the examination of aphasia and related disturbances.* New York: The Psychological Corporation, 1954.

Engelmann, S., & Bruner, E. C. *Distar reading I, II and III.* Chicago: Science Research Associates, 1969.

Ewing, A. W. G. *Aphasia in children.* Oxford: Oxford Medical Publications, 1930.

Eysenck, H. J., & Rachman, S. *The causes and cures of neurosis.* San Diego: Robert R. Knapp, 1965.

Ferinden, W. E. *Classroom management through the application of behavior modification techniques.* Linden, N.J.: Remediation Associates, 1970.

Fernald, G. M. *Remedial techniques in basic school subjects.* New York: McGraw-Hill, 1943.

Fletcher, H. L. Suggestions on correcting left-to-right reversals in reading and writing. In J. I. Arena (Ed.), *Teaching educationally handicapped children.* San Rafael, Calif.: Academic Therapy Publications, 1967.

Fries, C. G., Fries, A., Wilson, R., & Rudolph, M. *The Merrill linguistic readers.* Columbus, Ohio: Charles E. Merrill, 1966.

Frostig, M., Lefever, D. W., & Whittlesey, J. R. B., Maslow, P., *The Marianne Frostig developmental test of visual perception.* Palo Alto, Calif.: Consulting Psychologists Press, 1966.

Fuller, R. Breaking down the IQ walls: Severely retarded people *can* learn to read. *Psychology Today,* August 1974, pp. 96–102.

Fuller, R. *Ball-stick-bird readers* (Nos. 1–5). Available from Box 195, Owings Mills, MD 21117.

Gibson, E. J. Learning to read. In N. S. Endler *et al.* (Eds.), *Contemporary issues in developmental psychology.* New York: Holt, Rinehart & Winston, 1968.

Gillingham, A., & Stillman, B. W. *Remedial training for children with specific disability in reading, spelling, and penmanship.* Cambridge, Mass.: Educators Publishing Service, 1960.

Gnagey, W. J. *The psychology of discipline in the classroom.* New York: Macmillan, 1967.

Goodman, W. *A survival manual: Case studies and suggestions for the learning disabled teenager.* Yorktown Heights, New York: Board of Cooperative Educational Services, 1973.

Gray, J. *The teacher's survival guide* (Rev. ed.). Belmont, Calif.: Fearon Publishers, 1974.

Gray, J. *Teaching without tears: Your first year in the secondary school.* Belmont, Calif.: Fearon Publishers, 1968.

Greene, D., & Lepper, M. R. Intrinsic motivation: How to turn play into work. *Psychology Today,* August 1974, pp. 49–52.

Hammill, D. D. Training visual perception processes. *Journal of Learning Disabilities,* 1972, *5,* 552–559.

Hammill, D. D. & Larsen, S. C. The relationship of selected auditory perceptual skills and reading ability. *Journal of Learning Disabilities,* 1974, *7,* 40–46.

Heckelman, R. G. *Solutions to reading problems.* San Rafael, Calif.: Academic Therapy Publications, 1974.

Helms, H. B. An intermediate step in a total spelling program. In J. I. Arena (Ed.), *Building spelling skills in dyslexic children.* San Rafael, Calif.: Academic Therapy Publications, 1967.

Hill, W. F. *Learning: A survey of psychological interpretations.* San Francisco: Chandler, 1963.

Hiskey, M. S. *Books for slow readers.* Available from 5640 Baldwin, Lincoln, NB 68507, 1969.

Hoephner, R., Stern, C., & Nummedal, S. CSE-ERCC preschool/kindergarten test evaluation: UCLA graduate school of education, 1971.

Homme, L., Csanyi, A. P., Gonzales, M. A., & Rechs, J. R. *How to use contingency contracting in the classroom.* Champaign, Ill.: Research Press, 1970.

Hunter, M. *Reinforcement theory for teachers.* El Segundo, Calif.: Tip, 1967.

Jastak, J. F., & Jastak, S. R. *Manual of instructions, The wide range achievement test.* Wilmington, Del.: Guidance Associates, 1965.

Jenkins, J. R., Bausell, B. R., & Jenkins, L. M. Comparison of letter name and letter sound training as transfer variables. *American Educational Research Journal,* 1972, *9,* 75–86.

Johnson, D. L. Does perceptual training improve reading?—Another view. *Academic Therapy,* 1974, *10,* 65–68.

Johnson, J., & Myklebust, H. R. *Learning disabilities.* New York: Grune and Stratton, 1967.

Jordan, B. T. *Jordan left-right reversal test.* San Rafael, Calif.: Academic Therapy Publications, 1973.

Kahn, E. J. Handwriting and vision. In J. I. Arena (Ed.), *Building handwriting skills in dyslexic children.* San Rafael, Calif.: Academic Therapy Publications, 1970.

Kline, M. The new math: A passing aberration. *Learning,* February 1974, pp. 18–20.

Knox, G. M. (with E. Keisler). What do you do if your child can't learn? *Better Homes and Gardens,* September, 1974, pp. 40–46; 133.

Kost, M. L. *Success or failure begins in the early school years.* Springfield, Ill.: Charles C. Thomas, 1972.

Lindamood, C. H., & Lindamood, P. C. *A. D. D. program: Auditory discrimination in depth.* Boston: Teaching Resources Corporation, 1971.

Lindsley, D. B., & Henry, C. E. The effects of drugs on behavior and the electroencephalograms of children with behavior disorders. *Psychosomatic Medicine,* 1962, *4,* 140–49.

Lloyd, A. C., & Krevolin, N. *You learn to type.* New York: McGraw-Hill, 1966.

Luria, A. R. *Higher cortical functions in man.* New York: Basic Books, 1966.

Madsen, C. H., & Madsen, C. K. *Teaching discipline.* Boston: Allyn and Bacon, 1970.

Mann, L. Perceptual training: Misdirections and redirections. *American Journal of Orthopsychiatry,* 1970, *40,* 30–38.

McCarthy, J. J., & McCarthy, J. F. *Learning disabilities.* Boston: Allyn and Bacon, 1969.

Medical Economics. *Physicians' desk reference, 1973.* Oradell, N.J.: Author, 1972.

Money, J. On learning and not learning to read. In J. Money (Ed.), *The disabled reader.* Baltimore: The Johns Hopkins Press, 1966.

O'Halloran, G. *Teach yourself i. t. a.* Belmont, Calif.: Fearon Publishers, 1973.

Palkes, H., Stewart, M. A., & Kahana, B. Porteus maze performance of hyperactive boys after training in self-directed verbal commands. *Child Development,* 1968, *39,* 817–829.

Patterson, G. R., & Gullion, M. E. *Living with children.* Champaign, Ill.: Research Press, 1968.

Petitclerc, G. *Young fingers on a typewriter.* San Rafael, Calif.: Academic Therapy Publications, 1973.

Plunkett, M. B. *A writing manual for teaching the left-handed* and *Writing exercises for the left-handed.* Cambridge, Mass.: Educators Publishing Service, 1967.

Satz, P. and Friel, J. Some predictive antecedents of specific reading disability: A preliminary two-year follow-up. *Journal of Learning Disabilities,* 1974, *7,* 48–55.

Schrag, P. & Divoky, D. *The myth of the hyperactive child and other means of child control.* New York: Pantheon Books, 1975.

Simensen, R. J., & Sutherland, J. Psychological assessment of brain damage: the Wechsler scales. *Academic Therapy,* 1974, *10,* 69–81.

Slosson, R. L. *A game to improve your child's reading.* East Aurora, N.Y.: Slosson Educational Publications, 1963.

Van Riper, C. *Speech correction* (5th ed.). Englewood Cliffs, N.J.: Prentice-Hall, 1972.

Weiss, H. G., & Weiss, M. *A parents' and teachers' guide to learning disabilities.* Yorktown Heights, N.Y.: Board of Cooperative Educational Services, 1973.

Wiederholt, J. L. Interchange: The president of the CEC division for children with learning disabilities speaks out. *Journal of Learning Disabilities,* 1974, *7,* 508–512.

Zifferblatt, S. M. *Improving study and homework behaviors.* Champaign, Ill.: Research Press, 1970.

For Further Reading

The Definition of Learning Disability

Peskin, A., & Tauber-Scheidlinger, R., "Let them learn their way," *Academic Therapy*, 1976, *11*, 301–11.

The authors assert that learning disability may be more a matter of one child's style of learning than anything else.

Phipps, P. M., "Learning disabilities and teacher competencies," *Academic Therapy*, 1976–77, *12*, 225–30.

Sartain, H. W., "Instruction of disabled learners: a reading perspective," *Journal of Learning Disabilities*, 1976, *9*, 489–97.

Sartain leads off with the troubling point that the more money *for* LD-ism, the more LD-ism there is sure to be.

Sulzbacher, S., & Kenowitz, L., "At last, a definition of learning disabilities we can live with?" *Journal of Learning Disabilities*, 1977, *10*, 67–69.

The authors recommend the use of systematic observation and criterion-referenced measures to replace the use of global intelligence measures. They say: "There is a growing number of educators who maintain that children do not have learning disabilities but rather, schools have dyspedagogia."

History of LD-ism

Lilly, M., "A merger of the categories: are we finally ready?" *Journal of Learning Disabilities*, 1977, *10*, 115–21.

Lilly concludes that time spent in labeling children could better be spent in solving the more basic problems of instruction.

Wiederholt, J. L., "Historical perspectives on the education of the learning disabled," In J. Mann & D. Sabatino (eds.), *The second review of special education* (Philadelphia: J.S.E. Press, 1974).

General LD References

Asimov, I., "His own particular drummer," *Phi Delta Kappan,* 1976, *58,* 99–103.
Cruickshank, W. M., "Myths and realities in learning disabilities," *Journal of Learning Disabilities,* 1977, *10,* 51–58.

We do not agree with his insistence on a perceptual basis for LD-ism.

Hammill, D., & Bartel, N., *Teaching children with learning and behavioral problems* (Boston: Allyn and Bacon, 1975).
Ross, A. O., *Psychological aspects of learning disabilities and reading disorders* (New York: McGraw-Hill, 1976).

Perceptual Training

Hammill, D. D., & Wiederholt, J. L., "Review of the Frostig Visual Perception Test and the related training program," In J. Mann & D. Sabatino (eds.), *The first review of special education,* (Philadelphia: Buttonwood Farms, 1973).
Pitcher-Baker, G., "The Rosetta Stone revisited, or . . .?" *Academic Therapy,* 1976, *12,* 39–51.

She asks whether perceptual training improves reading but sounds a cautionary note before we reject it entirely.

Cursive Writing

Early, G. H., Nelson, D. A., Kleber, D. J., Tregoob, M., Huffman, E., & Cass, C., "Cursive handwriting, reading, and spelling achievement," *Academic Therapy,* 1976, *12,* 67–74.

The authors say that those taught cursive first may have fewer reading-spelling errors.

Color-Cuing

Goodman, M. D., & Cundick, B. P., "Learning rates with black and white letters," *Journal of Learning Disabilities*, 1976, *9*, 600–02.

Color-cuing of troublesome letters is shown in experiment to help in teaching them to LD children.

Typewriting

Miller, J., "Skill checklist," *Academic Therapy*, 1975–76, *11*, 243–49.

Preparation of Pupils for Testing

Miller, J., "Please clue them in," *Academic Therapy*, 1976–77, *12*, 231–34.

This article should be compulsory reading for all school system employees who work directly with children.

Troublesome Words in Reading

Allington, R. L., Gormley, K. & Truex, S., "Poor and normal readers' achievement on visual tasks involving high frequency, low discriminability words," *Journal of Learning Disabilities*, 1976, *9*, 292–96.

Here are the troublesome words. Drill on these with flash card practice and color-cuing:

went	where	was	that	on
than	they	want	of	for
when	were	but	saw	with
what	here	then	there	this

Right Brain/Left Brain

Brandwein, P., & Ornstein, R., "The duality of the mind," *Instructor*, January 1977, pp. 54–59.

Hunter, M., "Right-brained kids in left-brained schools," *The Education Digest*, February 1977, pp. 8–10.

High-Interest, Low-Vocabulary Books

Ekwall, E. E., *Locating and correcting reading difficulties* (Columbus, Ohio: Charles E. Merrill, 1970).

Ekwell's Appendix B lists specific high-interest, low-vocabulary books for reluctant readers from early grammar school to adult age levels. He also discusses games and game-like materials for building reading skills.

Index

Both Carlene T. Sampson, Ed.D. and Emmett C. Velten, Jr., Ph.D. have worked extensively with learning-disabled children. Dr. Sampson was a school psychologist in the Tucson and Yuma (Arizona) public schools, and Dr. Velten is a staff psychologist at the Yuma Guidance Center.